Akia's

Spiritual

Rituals

Akia's Spiritual Rituals

Akia

Copyright The Little French's Media LLC 2024

Published by Blue Dragoon Books

Cover Art by Blue Dragoon Books

This book guides you on a journey to discover your inherent strength. You'll learn how to harness your energy and channel it through powerful rituals, designed to awaken the potential within you.

However, true success lies not just in rituals, but in cultivating self-belief and aligning yourself with the universe's flow. This book provides the key to unlock your desires but emphasizes that it's a collaborative effort. The rituals act as catalysts, empowering you to take concrete actions and maintain a positive mindset, ultimately shaping your own destiny. Remember, these tools are meant to amplify your own will, not to manipulate or control others.

Who are you?

You are a being composed of three inseparable dimensions: body, mind, and spirit. This triad, also known as the physical, the non-physical, and the metaphysical, represents the very essence of your being. In Christian tradition, this trinity has been called the Holy Trinity, while other cultures and disciplines have conceptualized it in various ways.

A Reflection of Divinity

What transpires within you is also reflected in the nature of God. God manifests as a Triune being, a unity composed of three entities: Father, Son, and Holy Spirit. This analogy between the human and the divine has been recognized by various schools of thought.

Convergences in Different Disciplines

The concept of the three inseparable dimensions of the human being - body, mind, and spirit - has found parallels across various disciplines, each offering their unique perspectives on this fundamental aspect of human existence.

In the realm of psychiatry, this triumvirate has been termed the conscious, subconscious, and superconscious.

- The **conscious mind** encompasses our immediate awareness and thoughts, the aspects we readily access and control.
- The **subconscious mind**, often referred to as the "hidden mind," holds our memories, emotions, and experiences that lie beneath the surface of our conscious awareness.
- The **superconscious mind**, also known as the "higher mind," represents our connection to something greater than ourselves, a realm of intuition, inspiration, and spiritual awareness.

Philosophy, on the other hand, has conceptualized this triad as the id, ego, and superego.

- The **id** embodies our primal instincts and desires, the untamed drives that motivate our actions.

o   The **ego** serves as the mediator between the id and the superego, balancing our innate desires with societal norms and expectations.

o   The **superego** represents our internalized moral compass, the voice of conscience that guides our ethical behavior.

Even science has identified a similar triad in the physical world: energy, matter, and antimatter.

o   **Energy** is the capacity to do work, the intangible force that powers the universe.

o   **Matter** is the substance that makes up physical objects, the tangible elements that we can perceive and interact with.

o   **Antimatter** is the counterpart to matter, possessing the opposite electrical charge, and when matter and antimatter collide, they annihilate each other, releasing immense amounts of energy.

These examples demonstrate the remarkable convergence of this three-part structure across diverse fields of study, suggesting a fundamental pattern that permeates both the human experience and the physical universe. Whether it manifests as the conscious, subconscious, and superconscious mind, the id, ego, and superego, or energy, matter, and antimatter, this underlying triad seems to be a recurring theme in our understanding of reality.

The Three Energies That Shape Your Reality

The three dimensions of your being - body, mind, and spirit - are not merely abstract concepts; they manifest as **energies** that constantly interact with each other. You could call them **thought, word, and action**. The synergy of these three energies produces an outcome: what you know in your language and experience as **feeling** or **experience**.

How Do We Manifest?

The Symphony of Creation: Thought, Word, and Action

Thought is the initial note of creation, the silent melody that gives form to our ideas. But thought, on its own, remains in the realm of the intangible. For it to become something tangible, it must be expressed, it must **become word**.

The word, endowed with sound and vibration, possesses a dynamic power that surpasses that of mere thought. When spoken, the word releases a **creative energy** that expands through the universe, attracting and shaping reality around it. Words have the capacity to **transform**, **heal**, and even **destroy**, depending on the intention with which they are used.

But creation is not complete with the word. **Action** is the final chord, the materialization of the idea in the physical world. **Actions** are **words in motion**, the putting into practice of our thoughts and desires. It is through actions that we shape our destiny and leave our mark on the universe.

The Cycle of Creation: From God to Action and Back

The Source of Creation: Infinite Energy and Potential

At the heart of creation lies **God**, the boundless source of energy and potential. Through our thoughts, words, and actions, we partake in the divine creative process, co-creating our own reality.

The Culmination and Starting Point: Action

Action marks the culmination of this cycle, but it also serves as the starting point for a new creation. Each action we take generates new experiences, which in turn nourish our thoughts and words, propelling the creative cycle into an ascending spiral.

The Paradox of Asking: Releasing to Receive

Seeking what we desire might seem like a logical step towards attaining it. However, in reality, **asking from a place of lack only reinforces the feeling of not having**. The key to receiving lies in **releasing the need**, **trusting in the universe**, and **aligning ourselves with abundance**. When we focus on what we already possess and vibrate at the frequency of gratitude, we open the doors to the manifestation of our desires.

White Magic: A Path of Light and Harmony

The Essence of White Magic

White magic stands as the genuine and pure expression of magic, one that aligns perfectly with natural laws. Its essence lies in goodness, serving as a tool for our own well-being and that of others. Its power resides in kindness, completely avoiding any action that could cause harm or prejudice to another being. True magic reminds us that the power within us is not our own, but rather stems from a divine source. We are channels through which the divine will manifests in the world, always seeking good and harmony.

Key Principles of White Magic

1. **Alignment with Natural Laws:** White magic operates in harmony with the natural order of the universe, respecting the delicate balance of forces that govern existence.

2. **Benevolent Intention:** The guiding principle of white magic is unwavering benevolence, seeking the well-being of all beings without causing harm or infringement.

3. **Personal Empowerment:** White magic empowers individuals to tap into their inner potential and harness

their energy for positive transformation, both personal and collective.

4. **Conscious Connection:** White magic fosters a deep connection with the divine source, recognizing our role as conduits of divine energy in the world.

Applications of White Magic

1. **Healing and Wellness:** White magic can be employed to promote healing, both physical and emotional, by balancing energies and restoring harmony within the individual.

2. **Protection and Safeguarding:** White magic techniques can be used to create protective shields and ward off negative energies, ensuring safety and well-being.

3. **Spiritual Growth and Development:** White magic practices can facilitate spiritual growth and personal transformation, deepening one's connection to the divine and unlocking inner potential.

4. **Manifestation and Abundance:** White magic can be used to align with the flow of abundance, attracting positive experiences and opportunities into one's life.

Embrace the Path of White Magic

White magic invites us to embark on a journey of light and harmony, where we harness our inner power for the betterment of ourselves and the world around us. Through acts of kindness, compassion, and conscious connection, we can become agents of positive change, fostering a world filled with love, healing, and abundance.

The Power of the Mind:
The Foundation of White Magic

The Mind as the Crucible of Divine Power

At the heart of white magic lies the transformative power of our minds. The ability to focus and direct our thoughts is paramount, as they represent the expression of the divine power within us. However, the mind can be a double-edged sword, sometimes working against us in unconscious ways. This is why white magic encourages us to cultivate steadfast thoughts, imbued with faith and conviction in their physical manifestation. Vividly visualizing our desires and releasing them with trust in the universe is essential for allowing them to materialize in astonishing ways, aligning with the natural rhythm of the cosmos.

Harnessing the Power of Thought

1. **Conscious Awareness:** White magic emphasizes the importance of conscious awareness, enabling us to observe our thoughts and identify patterns that may hinder our progress.
2. **Focused Intention:** By cultivating unwavering focus, we can direct our mental energy towards our desired outcomes, increasing the likelihood of manifestation.

3. **Positive Affirmations:** Empowering affirmations, repeated with conviction, can help shape our beliefs and attract positive experiences into our lives.

4. **Creative Visualization:** Engaging in vivid mental imagery allows us to imprint our desires onto the fabric of reality, increasing their potential for manifestation.

5. **Detachment and Trust:** Once we have set our intentions in motion, white magic encourages us to detach from the outcome, trusting in the universe's unfolding plan.

Unleashing the Transformative Potential of White Magic

Through the mindful application of our mental faculties, white magic empowers us to:

1. **Heal and Harmonize:** We can promote healing, both physical and emotional, by balancing energies and restoring harmony within ourselves and others.

2. **Protect and Shield:** White magic techniques can be employed to create protective barriers and ward off negative energies, ensuring safety and well-being.

3. **Manifest Abundance:** We can align with the flow of abundance, attracting positive experiences and opportunities into our lives.

4. **Achieve Personal Growth:** White magic practices can facilitate spiritual growth and personal transformation,

deepening our connection to the divine and unlocking inner potential.

Embrace the Power of Your Mind

White magic invites us to recognize the extraordinary power of our minds, enabling us to shape our reality and manifest our deepest desires. By cultivating conscious awareness, focused intention, and unwavering faith, we can unlock the transformative potential of white magic, creating a life filled with love, healing, and abundance.

Trust and Detachment: Keys to Manifestation

Releasing Control and Embracing the Universe's Flow

Once we have set our intentions in motion by clearly and confidently expressing our thoughts, the next crucial step in manifestation is to **release** them and **trust** in the **universe**. This means letting go of the need to control the outcome and surrendering to the divine process of unfolding.

Why is Detachment Important?

1. **Aligning with the Universe's Rhythm:** The universe has its own unique rhythm and timing, often different from our own. By detaching from our desires, we allow the universe to manifest them in the most appropriate way and at the most opportune time.

2. **Preventing Negative Energy:** Anxiety, impatience, and doubt can create negative energy that hinders the manifestation process. Detachment helps us maintain a positive and open mindset, allowing our desires to flow freely.

3. **Cultivating Faith and Surrender:** Trusting in the universe requires faith in its benevolent and intelligent nature.

Detachment allows us to surrender our expectations and embrace the universe's infinite possibilities.

How to Practice Detachment

1. **Visualize and Affirm:** Clearly visualize your desired outcome and affirm it with conviction. Then, release the image and let go of the need to control how it manifests.

2. **Focus on Gratitude:** Shift your focus from what you want to what you already have. Expressing gratitude cultivates a positive mindset and aligns you with the frequency of abundance.

3. **Take Inspired Action:** While detachment emphasizes letting go of control, it doesn't mean being passive. Take inspired actions that align with your desires and trust that the universe will support your efforts.

4. **Observe and Learn:** Pay attention to synchronicities and signs that may indicate the universe's guidance. Learn from experiences, both positive and negative, and trust that they are part of your journey.

Remember, detachment is not about forgetting your desires; it's about releasing the need to control how they manifest. By trusting in the universe and embracing its flow, we open ourselves to the magic of manifestation and the fulfillment of our deepest aspirations.

Harnessing Nature's Power: Elements and Rituals

Nature's Embrace: A Source of Power and Harmony

White magic rituals find their primary source of support in the embrace of nature. The elements – fire, earth, air, and water– become powerful allies, each imbued with unique energies that enhance the manifestation process.

The Elements in Harmony

- **Fire:** Represented by candles, the element of fire brings warmth, passion, and transformation. It stimulates creativity, purification, and spiritual awakening.

- **Earth:** Symbolized by crystals, powders, and metals, the element of earth provides grounding, stability, and abundance. It anchors our intentions and connects us to the material world.

- **Air:** Present in prayers and invocations, the element of air represents communication, clarity, and mental power. It facilitates the exchange of ideas and the flow of inspiration.

- **Water:** Embodied in baths and cleansing rituals, the element of water signifies purification, healing, and emotional balance. It washes away negativity and opens us to new possibilities.

The Synergy of Elements in Rituals

By integrating these elements into rituals, we establish vibrational connections with the universe, harmonizing our inner world with the cosmic energy that surrounds us. The goal is to achieve a state of balance and alignment, allowing these energies to flow through our chakras – the energetic points that act as receptors of cosmic vibrations.

Benefits of Nature-Infused Rituals

- **Enhanced Manifestation:** The power of nature amplifies our intentions, increasing the likelihood of successful manifestation.

- **Personal Transformation:** Connecting with the elements fosters personal growth, spiritual awakening, and emotional well-being.

- **Healing and Harmony:** Nature's energies promote healing, both physical and emotional, restoring balance and vitality.

- **Deeper Connection with the Universe:** Rituals deepen our connection to the universe, fostering a sense of unity and belonging.

Embrace the Power of Nature

By incorporating nature's elements into your white magic rituals, you open yourself to a world of possibilities, where the power of the universe aligns with your intentions, leading to personal transformation, healing, and the manifestation of your deepest desires.

High Magic, Low Magic, and Hermetic Magic: A Journey Towards Spiritual Evolution

Magic, in its deepest essence, represents a path of transformation and self-discovery. However, there are different currents and approaches that define its practice and objectives.

High Magic

High Magic, also known as ceremonial magic, theurgy, or spiritual magic, is a complex and sophisticated system of practices aimed at achieving spiritual enlightenment and union with the divine. It is often associated with religious traditions, such as Western esotericism, Kabbalah, and Tantrism.

Low Magic

Low Magic, also known as folk magic, practical magic, or everyday magic, is a more down-to-earth approach to magic that focuses on using magical techniques to achieve practical goals in everyday life. It is often associated with folk traditions, such as herbalism, divination, and spellwork.

Hermetic Magic

Hermetic Magic, also known as the Hermetic Arts or the Western Esoteric Tradition, is a philosophical and practical system of magic that draws inspiration from ancient Egyptian and Greek sources. It is based on the belief that the universe is a unified whole, and that humans can access divine power through study, contemplation, and ritual practice.

The Journey Towards Spiritual Evolution

The practice of magic, regardless of its specific form, can be a powerful tool for personal and spiritual growth. It can help us to develop our intuition, connect with our inner power, and manifest our desires. However, it is important to remember that magic is not a shortcut to success or a way to control others. It is a journey of self-discovery and transformation that requires dedication, discipline, and a willingness to face our own shadows.

Additional Notes

- The terms "high magic" and "low magic" are often used in a hierarchical sense, with high magic being considered more spiritual and elevated than low magic. However, it is important to remember that both forms of magic have their own value and can be effective in achieving their respective goals.

- Hermetic Magic is a distinct tradition that encompasses both high and low magic practices. It is based on a specific set of philosophical principles and practices that are not shared by all other forms of magic.
- The journey towards spiritual evolution is a lifelong process. There is no destination, only the ongoing process of learning, growing, and transforming.

High Magic: The Path to Spiritual Evolution

High Magic, also known as white magic, is characterized by its pursuit of the individual's spiritual evolution. It focuses on developing mental, psychic, and spiritual abilities, utilizing tools such as meditation, visualization, prayer, and work with subtle energies. Its ultimate goal is to attain a state of higher consciousness, enlightenment, and connection with the divine.

Key Principles of High Magic:

1. **Self-Mastery:** High Magic emphasizes personal growth and transformation, requiring dedication, discipline, and a willingness to confront one's inner shadows.
2. **Connection to Higher Powers:** It seeks to establish a connection with a higher power, whether it be a specific deity, a universal force, or one's own higher self.

3. **Energetic Manipulation:** High Magic practitioners learn to harness and manipulate subtle energies to influence their inner and outer realities.

4. **Symbolic Language and Ritual:** Rituals, symbols, and sacred language play a significant role in High Magic, serving as tools for focus, intention, and connection to higher realms.

Practices of High Magic:

1. **Meditation:** Cultivating stillness and mindfulness to enhance self-awareness, connect with inner guidance, and access higher states of consciousness.

2. **Visualization:** Using mental imagery to create desired outcomes, reinforce intentions, and connect with symbolic archetypes.

3. **Prayer and Devotion:** Invoking divine energies, expressing gratitude, and seeking guidance through prayer, affirmations, and devotional practices.

4. **Energy Work:** Directing and manipulating subtle energies, such as Reiki or pranayama, to heal, balance, and transform oneself and others.

The Path of Spiritual Evolution:

High Magic is not a quick fix or a means to control external circumstances. It is a lifelong journey of self-discovery, spiritual growth, and alignment with one's higher purpose. It requires patience, perseverance, and a genuine desire to connect with something greater than oneself.

As one progresses on this path, they may experience:

1. **Enhanced Intuition:** Increased ability to perceive subtle energies, insights, and guidance from within and from higher realms.

2. **Expanded Consciousness:** A broader perspective on reality, deeper understanding of oneself and the universe, and a connection to the interconnectedness of all things.

3. **Personal Transformation:** Overcoming limiting beliefs, healing emotional wounds, and developing positive qualities such as compassion, love, and wisdom.

4. **Connection to the Divine:** Experiencing a profound sense of unity with a higher power, a feeling of being part of something larger and more meaningful.

High Magic offers a profound path for those seeking spiritual evolution and a deeper connection with the divine. It is a journey of self-discovery, transformation, and alignment with one's true purpose in life.

Low Magic: Seeking Material Goals

In contrast, Low Magic, also known as black magic, focuses on achieving material or worldly goals. Rituals and spells are employed to attain objectives such as love, wealth, protection, or power. However, this stream can have negative consequences if not practiced responsibly and ethically.

Key Principles of Low Magic:

1. **Goal-Oriented:** Low Magic is driven by specific desires and objectives, seeking tangible outcomes in the physical world.

2. **Practical Application:** It utilizes practical techniques and tools, such as herbs, candles, and symbols, to influence the desired outcome.

3. **Energetic Manipulation:** Low Magic practitioners may manipulate energies, such as personal will or planetary influences, to achieve their goals.

4. **Ritual and Spellwork:** Rituals and spells form the core of Low Magic, providing a structured framework for channeling intent and energy.

Practices of Low Magic:

1. **Spellwork:** Crafting and performing spells that combine ingredients, symbols, and incantations to direct energy towards specific goals.

2. **Divination:** Using tools such as tarot cards, astrology, or runes to gain insights into situations and make informed decisions.

3. **Herbalism:** Utilizing the healing and magical properties of herbs for various purposes, such as protection, love, or prosperity.

4. **Sigil Magic:** Creating and empowering sigils, which are symbols imbued with specific intent, to attract desired energies.

Potential Consequences of Low Magic:

1. **Unintended Outcomes:** If not practiced with care, Low Magic can lead to unintended consequences, such as attracting negative energies or harming oneself or others.

2. **Karmic Repercussions:** Actions performed through Low Magic can have karmic implications, requiring careful consideration of ethical principles.

3. **Dependency on External Forces:** Overreliance on Low Magic for achieving goals can create a sense of dependency, hindering personal growth and empowerment.

Responsible and Ethical Practice:

1. **Clear Intentions:** Establish clear and positive intentions before engaging in any Low Magic practice.
2. **Respectful Approach:** Respect the free will of others and avoid manipulating or harming them for personal gain.
3. **Balance with Personal Effort:** Combine Low Magic with personal effort and dedication to achieve sustainable results.
4. **Seek Guidance:** Seek guidance from experienced practitioners or mentors to ensure responsible and ethical practices.

Low Magic, when approached with awareness, responsibility, and ethical considerations, can be a powerful tool for achieving personal goals and manifesting desired outcomes. However, it is crucial to recognize that it is not a substitute for personal effort, self-reflection, and alignment with one's values.

Hermetic Magic: Transcending the Material

Hermetic Magic, on the other hand, seeks to achieve its results solely through mental, psychic, and spiritual evolution. This stream, based on the principles of alchemy and astrology, considers that power lies in the mind and the ability to connect with universal energies.

Key Principles of Hermetic Magic:

1. **Mental Mastery:** Hermetic Magic emphasizes the development of mental faculties, including focus, concentration, and willpower.

2. **Energetic Connection:** It seeks to establish a connection with universal energies, cosmic forces, and the subtle energies that permeate the universe.

3. **Symbolic Understanding:** Symbols, archetypes, and sacred language play a significant role in Hermetic Magic, serving as keys to unlocking deeper understanding and transformation.

4. **Personal Transformation:** The ultimate goal of Hermetic Magic is personal transformation, leading to a state of higher consciousness, enlightenment, and alignment with one's true purpose.

Practices of Hermetic Magic:

1. **Meditation and Contemplation:** Cultivating stillness and mindfulness to enhance self-awareness, connect with inner guidance, and access higher states of consciousness.

2. **Alchemy:** Utilizing alchemical principles and practices, both symbolically and physically, to transform oneself and one's experiences.

3. **Astrology:** Studying and understanding astrological influences to gain insights into oneself, the universe, and the timing of events.

4. **Ritual and Symbolism:** Engaging in sacred rituals and using symbolic language to focus intention, connect with higher realms, and facilitate transformation.

Magic as a Tool for Transformation:

Regardless of the stream followed, the practice of magic involves a profound inner journey. As one delves into this world, they experience a transformation in their perspective on life, developing a greater awareness of themselves, the universe, and their own potential.

Benefits of Magical Practice:

1. **Enhanced Self-Awareness:** Increased understanding of one's thoughts, emotions, motivations, and connection to the world around them.

2. **Expanded Consciousness:** A broader perspective on reality, deeper understanding of oneself and the universe, and a connection to the interconnectedness of all things.

3. **Personal Transformation:** Overcoming limiting beliefs, healing emotional wounds, and developing positive qualities such as compassion, love, and wisdom.

4.   **Connection to the Divine:** Experiencing a profound sense of unity with a higher power, a feeling of being part of something larger and more meaningful.

Magic, when approached with a sincere desire for self-discovery, transformation, and connection with the divine, can offer a powerful path for personal growth and spiritual evolution. It is a journey of self-mastery, alignment with one's true purpose, and the realization of one's full potential.

The Awakening of the Magical Being

As an individual embarks on the magical path, they embark on a journey of self-discovery, uncovering the **magical being** that resides within. This being represents the boundless potential that each person possesses to **shape their own destiny** and achieve their deepest aspirations.

Distinguishing the Paths of Magic:

1.   **High Magic:** Embraces spiritual evolution, seeking enlightenment and connection with the divine.
2.   **Low Magic:** Pursues material goals, utilizing magic to manifest desired outcomes in the physical world.
3.   **Hermetic Magic:** Transcends the material, focusing on mental, psychic, and spiritual transformation.
4.

The Transformative Power of Magic:

Engaging in magical practices initiates a profound inner journey, fostering a transformation in one's perspective on life. It cultivates:

1. **Enhanced Self-Awareness:** A deeper understanding of one's thoughts, emotions, motivations, and connection to the world around them.
2. **Expanded Consciousness:** A broader perspective on reality, a deeper understanding of oneself and the universe, and a connection to the interconnectedness of all things.
3. **Personal Transformation:** The ability to overcome limiting beliefs, heal emotional wounds, and develop positive qualities such as compassion, love, and wisdom.
4. **Connection to the Divine:** A profound sense of unity with a higher power, a feeling of being part of something larger and more meaningful.

The Magical Being: Unveiling Inner Potential:

The **magical being** represents the boundless potential that lies dormant within each individual. It is the source of:

1. **Unwavering Willpower:** The ability to focus intention, overcome obstacles, and persevere in the face of challenges.

2. **Creative Power:** The capacity to manifest desired outcomes, shape one's reality, and bring dreams to fruition.

3. **Intuitive Wisdom:** The ability to access inner guidance, make informed decisions, and navigate life's complexities with clarity.

4. **Unconditional Love:** The capacity to extend compassion, understanding, and acceptance to oneself and others.

Reflections on the Magical Journey:

The original text provides a comprehensive overview of the diverse streams of magic. The enhanced version strives to preserve the essence of the original message while employing clearer and more accessible language. It incorporates metaphors and examples to facilitate comprehension and enriches the text with elements such as the concept of the **magical being**. The original structure of the text is maintained to enhance readability and understanding.

Ultimately, the path of magic is a personal and transformative journey, empowering individuals to uncover their true potential, shape their destinies, and connect with the profound wisdom and power that lies within.

Manifest Your Dreams with This Powerful Ritual

This experiment guides you through a manifestation process to attract a desire that you truly yearn for, as long as it is in harmony with yourself and the world, without negatively affecting others.

Follow these steps to materialize it:

1. **Define your desire clearly and in detail:**

- Choose a deep desire, something you passionately crave.
- Ensure that your desire is aligned with your well-being and that of others.
- Write it down on a sheet of paper, describing it in great detail. Don't focus on how to get it, just on how it would be if you already had it.
- If it is an object, describe its color, texture, smell, etc.
- If it is a situation, detail how you would feel, what people would be present, etc.
- As you write, visualize your desire as if it had already been fulfilled. Feel the emotion of having it and the gratitude towards the universe.

2.   **Connect with your desire every night:**

- Keep the sheet with you in a special place.
- Read your desire aloud every night before bed.
- Feel the emotion of having it as you read.
- Trust that your desire will be fulfilled and thank the universe for it.

3.   **Celebrate the manifestation:**

- When your desire comes true, burn the sheet as a symbol of gratitude.
- Express gratitude to the universe for its collaboration.

Additional tips:

- Repeat this experiment with different desires.
- Be patient and consistent. Manifestation can take time.
- Don't give up if you don't see immediate results. Maintain faith and trust.
- Visualize your desire frequently, even outside of the experiment.
- Surround yourself with positive emotions such as joy, gratitude, and hope.
- Be careful with your thoughts. Do not feed doubts or fears, as these can block manifestation.

Remember: This experiment is a powerful tool to attract your desires, but it requires your commitment and energy. Believe in yourself, in the power of the universe, and in the magic of attraction.

I wish you much success in manifesting your desires!

How to Visualize a Desire

Strengthen your mental power and attract your desires with this powerful visualization technique

This exercise complements the one with the written sheet, providing you with an additional tool to materialize your dreams. Do it first thing in the morning, when you wake up, dedicating only five minutes a day to it.

Preparation:

- Find a **quiet place** where you will not be interrupted.
- Sit in a chair with your back straight, maintaining a comfortable posture.
- Place your hands on your legs in a relaxed position.
- Close your eyes and take a few deep breaths, inhaling through your nose and exhaling through your mouth.
- Let your mind free itself from thoughts and worries.
- Imagine a **white or serene space** in your mind.

Visualization of desire:

- When you feel your mind calm, visualize your desire as if you have already achieved it.
- Create a **mental movie** in the present tense, as if it were a tangible reality.

- Feel the **emotions** that would invade you when you have fulfilled your desire.

- Observe the **details** as precisely as possible: colors, textures, sounds, people involved, etc.

- Allow the image to form in your mind **without forcing it**. Let it flow naturally.

- Don't worry if the image is not clear at first. With practice, it will get stronger.

- When the image is clear in your mind, visualize it ascending into the sky as if you were planting it in the universe.

- **Thank the universe** for the manifestation of your desire.

Additional recommendations:

- Do not think or talk about your desire during the day, except when reading the sheet at night.

- Practice this visualization daily to strengthen its effect.

- Combine this technique with writing the sheet to enhance results.

- Maintain a **positive and confident attitude**. Believe in the power of visualization and in the manifestation of your desires.

- Train your mind to focus on the present. Observe your surroundings with attention and live in the here and now.

- This practice will improve your concentration and visualization power.

Remember: The key to success lies in **consistency, faith, and clear visualization**. Dedicate time each day to this exercise and don't get discouraged if you don't see immediate results. Trust in the power of your mind and in the magic of the universe to attract your deepest desires.

I wish you much luck on this path of transformation and manifestation!

LOVE
RITUALS

White Magic Spell to Strengthen Love

Ingredients:

- A plain glass
- Water (to fill three-quarters of the glass)
- A tablespoon of sugar
- A photograph of your loved one
- A small spoon

Preparation:

1. Perform this spell during the waxing moon, after consulting the lunar calendar.
2. Place the photograph of your loved one on a flat surface.
3. Place the glass of water on top of the photograph.
4. Add the tablespoon of sugar to the water and stir with the small spoon until it dissolves completely.
5. While stirring the sugar, recite the following prayer aloud and with conviction, repeating it three times:

(Name of your loved one), may sweetness and tenderness reign in our relationship. May the problems between us dissipate and our love grow stronger and stronger each day.

6. Continue stirring the water with the small spoon while visualizing your relationship with your loved one filled with love, harmony, and happiness.

7. Repeat this spell daily, preferably during the day and under sunlight.

8. At the end of each day, pour the water used in the spell onto the earth, not anywhere else.

Recommendations:

- You can repeat this spell as many times as you wish until you achieve the desired result.

- Remember that the key to making this spell work is to perform it with faith, conviction, and clearly visualizing the result you want to obtain.

- This spell is simple, yet very effective in strengthening love and unity in a couple facing communication or discord issues.

Important:

- Keep in mind that this spell does not replace open and honest dialogue with your partner to resolve any problems that may exist in the relationship.
- White magic seeks well-being and harmony through positive energy, so it should always be performed with good intentions and without any kind of resentment or negativity.

Rekindle the Flame of Love:
A Ritual to Win Back Your Partner

Materials:

- Seven plain red candles
- A fountain pen with red ink
- A white sheet of paper divided into seven parts
- A base for placing the candle
- An ashtray

Preparation:

1. Choose a quiet and private place where you can perform the ritual without interruptions.
2. Make sure you have all the materials on hand before you begin.
3. Start the ritual on a New Moon Friday.

Ritual Steps:

1. **Petition:** On each of the seven parts of the white paper, write the name of the person you want to win back with the red pen. In the last part, write your own name.
2. **Magic phrase:** On the same sheet of paper, write the following phrase in red ink: "You and I will remain united. If our love is fading, the flame of this candle will help me illuminate your mind so that you will not leave me, and we will continue together forever. So be it and so it must be."
3. **Lighting the candle:** Light one of the red candles and place the sheet of paper on the base, allowing the flame to consume the written petition.
4. **Contemplation:** As the candle burns, observe the flame and visualize the connection you want to rekindle with your partner. Focus on the feelings of love and union that once united you.

5. **Burning the paper:** Once the candle has burned for about an hour, extinguish the flame and let the paper burn completely in the ashtray.

6. **Sealing the ritual:** Collect the ashes of the paper and scatter half in a flowerpot or in a park. Say the name of the person as you scatter the ashes. Keep the other half of the ashes in a safe place like a small reliquary.

7. **Repetition:** Repeat this ritual for the next six Fridays, using a new candle each time.

Recommendations:

- Perform the ritual with faith and conviction.
- Clearly visualize the love you want to rekindle.
- Express your desires with sincerity and emotion.
- Maintain a positive attitude throughout the process.

Remember:

This ritual is a tool that can help you reconnect with your partner, but its success depends largely on your own effort and commitment. It is important to work on healing past wounds and building a strong relationship based on respect, communication, and mutual love.

Considerations:

It is important to note that this ritual is not a magical solution to couple problems. If you are going through a difficult situation with your partner, I recommend that you seek professional help from a psychologist or therapist. A specialist can help you identify the underlying problems and find solutions that are right for your particular case.

Saint Anthony's Love Binding:
A Ritual to Attract the Desired Love

Materials:

- An image of Saint Anthony (preferably gifted)
- A dirty garment of the person you want to conquer
- A photo of the same person
- A regular-sized clay pot
- A novena to Saint Anthony

Preparation:

1. **Choose the right day:** Perform the ritual on a Thursday, the day dedicated to Saint Anthony, preferably during the waning moon.

2. **Gather the materials:** Make sure you have all the necessary elements before you begin.

Ritual Steps:

1. **Symbolic union:** Wrap the image of Saint Anthony with the dirty garment of the person you want to conquer. This represents the symbolic union you want to create.

2. **Image placement:** Place the wrapped image of Saint Anthony upside down inside the clay pot. This symbolizes the attraction you want to exert on the person.

3. **Sealing the ritual:** Cover the clay pot completely so that no light enters. This seals the energy of the ritual and protects its intention.

4. **Novena prayer:** For nine consecutive days, pray the novena to Saint Anthony with devotion and faith. Ask the saint to intercede for you and help you win the love of the desired person.

5. **Visualization and concentration:** While you pray, clearly visualize the image of the person you want to conquer next to you, in a loving and happy relationship. Focus on the feelings of love and union that would unite you.

6. **Patience and persistence:** Have patience and faith during the process. It is important that you continue to

pray the novena each day, even if you do not see immediate results.

7. **Undoing the ritual:** Once you have achieved your goal, you can undo the ritual. Remove the image of Saint Anthony from the pot and burn the dirty garment. Wash the clay pot and store it in a safe place.

Recommendations:

- Perform the ritual in a quiet and private place where you can concentrate without interruptions.
- Have faith and conviction in the power of the ritual.
- Clearly visualize the love you want to conquer.
- Express your desires with sincerity and emotion.
- Maintain a positive attitude throughout the process.

Considerations:

It is important to note that this ritual is a tool that can help you attract the love of the desired person, but its success depends largely on your own effort and commitment. It is important that you work on your self-esteem and personal development to be an attractive and magnetic person. In addition, remember that true love is based on respect, communication, and mutual understanding.

Warning:

This ritual should not be used to manipulate or control another person. True love is based on free will and mutual respect. If your intention is to harm or hurt someone, this ritual will not give you the results you desire.

Capture Their Thoughts:
A Ritual to Occupy Someone's Mind

Materials:

- Twenty-one plain white candles
- A new knife
- Honey
- Cinnamon powder
- A pencil

Preparation:

- **Choose the location:** Perform the ritual in a quiet and private place where you can concentrate without interruptions.
- **Gather the materials:** Make sure you have all the necessary items before you begin.

Steps of the ritual:

1. **Engraving on the candle:** With the pencil, write vertically on the candle the name of the person you want to enchant. Then, write your name horizontally above the person's name.

2. **Enchanting with the knife:** Take the new knife and prick the candle while saying aloud: "[Person's name], you will not be able to rest, and you will not be able to get my image out of your mind." Clearly visualize the image of the person occupied by your thoughts.

3. **Anointing with honey and cinnamon:** Anoint the candle with honey and sprinkle with cinnamon powder. The honey represents the attraction you want to generate, while the cinnamon symbolizes the power and magic of the ritual.

4. **Lighting and prayer:** Light the candle and repeat the prayer three times with faith and conviction: "[Person's name], you will not be able to rest, and you will not be able to get my image out of your mind." Visualize the connection you want to create with the person.

5. **Complete consumption:** Let the candle burn completely. This represents the intensity and duration of the effect you want to achieve.

6.   **Repeat for 21 days:** Repeat this ritual for twenty-one consecutive days, lighting a new candle each day. It is not necessary to wait for the previous candle to burn completely before lighting the next one.

Recommendations:

- Perform the ritual with faith and conviction.
- Clearly visualize the image of the person occupied by your thoughts.
- Express your desires with sincerity and emotion.
- Maintain a positive attitude throughout the process.

Considerations:

It is important to keep in mind that this ritual is a tool that can help you occupy the mind of the desired person, but the success of it depends largely on your own effort and commitment. It is important that you work on your self-esteem and personal development to be an attractive and magnetic person. Also, remember that true love is based on respect, communication, and mutual understanding.

Warning:

This ritual should not be used to manipulate or control another person. True love is based on free will and mutual respect. If your intention is to harm or hurt someone, this ritual will not give you the results you want.

Harmonize Your Marriage:
A Ritual to Strengthen Your Bond

Materials:

- None specific, just the presence of the couple and their willingness to participate.

Preparation:

- **Choose the location:** Perform the ritual on a quiet beach, preferably at sunset or at night. The sound of the sea and the energy of the moon will create a conducive environment for connection.
- **Connect with your partner:** It is important that both of you are present at the ritual, with open minds and willing to strengthen your bond.

Steps of the ritual:

1. **Joint declaration:** Holding hands, say aloud with conviction the following phrase: "May all that is bad and negative be removed from us two (say your names)."

Visualize together the negative energy moving away from your relationship.

2. **Affirmation of strength:** Repeat aloud: "There will be no problems that we as a couple cannot overcome (repeat your names)." Trust in your strength as a team and in your ability to overcome any obstacle.

3. **Promise of eternal union:** Declare with emotion: "Our lives will be united forever and nothing and no one will be able to separate us, only God." Visualize your future together, full of love, support, and happiness.

4. **Seal with power:** Finish by saying with conviction: "From our word, so shall be the power." Feel the energy of your commitment flowing between you.

5. **Connection with the sea:** Enter the sea hand in hand and walk together along the shore seven times. Recite the entire prayer aloud on each occasion: "May all that is bad and negative be removed from us two (say your names)... From our word, so shall be the power." Feel the energy of the sea purifying your relationship and strengthening your bond.

Recommendations:

- Perform the ritual with faith and conviction.
- Visualize together the harmony and love you want to cultivate in your marriage.
- Express your desires with sincerity and emotion.

- Maintain a positive and committed attitude towards your relationship.

Considerations:

It is important to keep in mind that this ritual is a tool that can help you strengthen your marriage, but its success depends largely on your own effort and commitment. Open communication, mutual respect, and a willingness to work together are fundamental pillars for a healthy and lasting relationship.

Warning:

This ritual should not be used as a magical solution to marital problems. If you are going through a crisis in your relationship, I recommend that you seek professional help from a couples therapist. A specialist can help you identify the underlying problems and find solutions that are appropriate for your specific case.

Peace and Happiness with Your Partner:
A Ritual to Strengthen Harmony

Materials:

- A long blue candle
- Pure honey
- A pencil

Preparation:

- **Choose the location:** Perform the ritual in a quiet and private place where you can concentrate without interruptions.
- **Gather the materials:** Make sure you have all the necessary items before you begin.

Steps of the ritual:

1. **Engraving of names:** With the pencil, write along the length of the candle, starting from the wick, your name and then the name of your loved one. Visualize the connection of love and harmony you want to create with them.

2. **Anointing with honey:** Anoint a small portion of the candle with pure honey. The honey represents the sweetness and attraction you want to draw into your relationship.

3. **Lighting and prayer:** Light the candle and say the following phrase with faith and conviction: "(The name of your partner), you and I will be happy, we will always have peace and love. Anger will not blind our minds and we will both avoid arguments when they arise." Visualize a future full of peace, understanding, and love with your partner.

4. **Extinguishing with saliva:** Let the candle burn for nine minutes. Then, extinguish it with your fingers moistened with saliva. The saliva symbolizes the union and commitment you want to strengthen with your partner.

5. **Repeat for three months:** Repeat this ritual for three consecutive months, starting on a Friday when you get out of bed. You can perform it in any lunar phase, but if you prefer, do it during the waxing moon to enhance its effect.

Additional considerations:

- Make sure the candle is smooth and of good quality.
- Perform the ritual with faith and conviction, believing in the power of your words and actions.
- Clearly visualize the peace, happiness, and harmony you want to create in your relationship.
- Maintain a positive and committed attitude towards your partner.

Recommendations:

In addition to the ritual, it is important that you work on strengthening your relationship on a daily basis. Some actions you can take are:

- **Open and honest communication:** Talk to your partner about your feelings, needs, and expectations. Listen to them attentively and empathetically.
- **Mutual respect:** Treat your partner with respect, even in moments of disagreement. Avoid hurtful words or destructive criticism.
- **Quality time together:** Dedicate quality time to be with your partner, without distractions. Share activities that you enjoy together and talk about topics that interest you.
- **Gratitude and affection:** Express your gratitude for your partner and the good things they bring to you. Show your affection with words, gestures, and loving actions.
- **Commitment and effort:** True love requires commitment and effort from both of you. Work together to find solutions to problems that may arise and be understanding and patient with each other.

Remember:

This ritual is a tool that can help you strengthen peace and happiness in your relationship, but its success depends largely on your own effort and commitment. True love is based on respect, communication, trust, and mutual support. If you are going through a crisis in your relationship, I recommend that you seek professional help from a couples therapist. A specialist can help you identify the underlying problems and find solutions that are appropriate for your specific case.

Bring Back Your Loved One: A Ritual to Rekindle Love

Materials:

- A green bottle
- A red ink pen
- A piece of white paper
- A long white candle
- Water

Preparation:

- **Choose the location:** Perform the ritual in a quiet and private place where you can concentrate without interruptions.
- **Gather the materials:** Make sure you have all the necessary items before you begin.

Steps of the ritual:

1. **Bottle preparation:** Fill the green bottle with water up to three-quarters full.

2. **Petition on paper:** On the white paper, write with the red pen the full name of the person you want to return to your side. Clearly visualize the image of that person and the connection you want to rekindle.

3. **Union with the candle:** Place the white candle on the top of the bottle. The candle represents the light of love that you want to ignite in the heart of your loved one.

4. **Lighting and prayer:** Light the candle and say aloud the following prayer with faith and conviction: "In the name of the Father, the Son, and the Holy Spirit, [name of the person] may the water bring you back to me, may the fire rekindle your love for me, and may the wind make you remember me always." Feel how the energy of the ritual begins to flow.

5. **Recite the Our Father:** Pray three Our Fathers with devotion, asking for the restoration of love and harmony in your relationship.

6. **Bottle placement:** Place the bottle in a corner of your room, in a safe place where it will not be disturbed. Let the candle burn completely.

7. **Repeat the ritual:** The next day, light another new white candle on the bottle and repeat the prayer and the rosary. It is not necessary to change the water or paper.

8.   **Auspicious days:** It is recommended to start this ritual on the 6th, 9th, or 12th of the month, at 3:00 in the morning. These days are considered auspicious for attraction and love.

Recommendations:

- Perform the ritual with faith and conviction.
- Clearly visualize the return of your loved one and the rekindling of love between you.
- Express your desires with sincerity and emotion.
- Maintain a positive attitude throughout the process.
- Be patient and trust in the power of the ritual.

Considerations:

It is important to keep in mind that this ritual is a tool that can help you rekindle the love of the person you desire, but its success depends largely on your own effort and commitment. True love is based on respect, communication, trust, and mutual support. If your intention is to manipulate or control the other person, this ritual will not give you the results you want.

Warning:

This ritual should not be used to harm or hurt anyone. True love is based on free will and mutual respect. If your intention is to harm or hurt the other person, this ritual will not give you the results you want.

Remember:

This ritual is a tool that can help you rekindle love, but the real work is up to you. Reflect on your relationship and find ways to improve it. Open communication, mutual respect, and joint effort are keys to a healthy and lasting relationship.

Spices to Increase Love Passion: A Ritual to Ignite the Fire

Materials:

- 4 inches of white silk
- 8 inches of narrow red ribbon
- 2 tablespoons of basil
- 2 tablespoons of black peppercorns
- 1 tablespoon of ground garlic
- 1 tablespoon of ground red pepper
- 1 tablespoon of ground oregano
- White thread

Preparation:

Choose the time: Perform the ritual on the first full moon of the month. The full moon represents feminine energy and fertility, favoring attraction and passion.

Making the bag: With the white silk, make a bag 3 inches wide by 4 inches long. Sew the bag with the white thread, focusing on the energy of the passion you want to attract.

Activation ritual: Tie the bag with the red ribbon and keep it for seven days in the drawer of your nightstand, near your bed. Visualize how the energy of passion intensifies in your room and in your relationship.

Spice mixture: After seven days, combine the basil, black pepper, oregano, ground red pepper, and ground garlic in a small bowl. Visualize how these spices represent the fire and intensity you want to awaken in your partner.

Filling the bag: Put the spice mixture inside the silk bag. Feel how the energy of passion concentrates in this little magical object.

Placement of the bag: Place the bag in your kitchen, in a visible and accessible place. The kitchen represents fire and transformation, so it is an ideal place to enhance the energy of passion.

Recommendations:

- Perform the ritual with faith and conviction.
- Clearly visualize the passion you want to ignite in your partner.
- Express your desires with sensuality and emotion.
- Maintain a positive and receptive attitude towards the energy of the ritual.

Use of spices:

- It is recommended to use a pinch of the spice mixture to season red meats. Red meat symbolizes passion and sensuality.
- You can experiment with the spice mixture in other recipes, always keeping in mind that it is a strong formula and should be used in moderation.

Considerations:

It is important to keep in mind that this ritual is a tool that can help you increase passion in your relationship, but its success depends largely on your own effort and commitment. Open communication, physical and emotional intimacy, and mutual effort to keep the flame of love alive are keys to a passionate and lasting relationship.

Warning:

This ritual should not be used to manipulate or control your partner. True passion is based on free will, mutual respect, and a genuine desire to share intimate and pleasurable moments. If your intention is to harm or hurt your partner, this ritual will not give you the results you want.

Remember:

Spices can be a magical ingredient to ignite passion in your relationship, but the real secret lies in cultivating love, trust, and communication on a daily basis.

Awaken Passion:
A Ritual to Ignite the Fire of Love

Materials:

- A small turkey bone
- A small cone of yarn
- Seven cilantro seeds
- Seven red rose petals

- A sheet of red cellophane paper

Preparation:

Choose the time: Perform the ritual on the first day of the new moon. The new moon represents the beginning of a new cycle, ideal for attracting the energy of love and passion.

Cone preparation: Inside the yarn cone, place the turkey bone, cilantro seeds, and red rose petals. Visualize how these elements come together to create a powerful energy of attraction and passion.

Wrapped in cellophane: Wrap the cone with the red cellophane paper, sealing the energy inside it. The color red symbolizes passion, love, and vitality.

Placement on the pillow: Place the cellophane-wrapped cone under your pillow, on the side where you sleep. Feel how the energy of the ritual begins to flow into your relationship.

Words of power:

As you place the cone under the pillow, recite the following phrase with conviction: "When we are together, your passion ignites, your love grows stronger every day, our bodies melt into the great bonfire of passion." Clearly visualize the passionate connection you want to create with your partner.

Recommendations:

- Perform the ritual with faith and conviction.
- Clearly visualize the passion you want to awaken in your partner.
- Express your desires with sensuality and emotion.
- Maintain a positive and receptive attitude towards the energy of the ritual.

Considerations:

It is important to keep in mind that this ritual is a tool that can help you awaken passion in your relationship, but its success depends largely on your own effort and commitment. Open communication, physical and emotional intimacy, and mutual effort to keep the flame of love alive are keys to a passionate and lasting relationship.

Warning:

This ritual should not be used to manipulate or control your partner. True passion is based on free will, mutual respect, and a genuine desire to share intimate and pleasurable moments. If your intention is to harm or hurt your partner, this ritual will not give you the results you want.

Remember:

The cone under the pillow can be a magical symbol to remind you of the power of passion in your relationship, but the real secret lies in cultivating love, trust, and communication on a daily basis.

To Recover a Loved One:
A Ritual to Rekindle the Connection

Materials:

- A virgin wax candle
- Nine red-headed pins
- A pencil

Preparation:

Choose the location: Perform the ritual in a quiet and private place where you can concentrate without interruptions.

Candle preparation: With the pencil, mark the candle into nine equal parts. Each part represents one day of the ritual.

Lighting the candle: Light the candle with your left hand. The left hand is associated with intuition and receptive energy.

Inserting the pins: Hold the candle firmly with your left hand and, with your right hand, stick a red-headed pin into the first marked part of the candle. Clearly visualize the image of the person you want to recover and the connection you want to rekindle with them.

Words of power: Speak the following phrase clearly and firmly: "The wax is more resistant than the will of [name of loved one] and that is why I order you to come and do not stop, to be restless wherever you are; you will come in body and soul to see me; because I order you and so it must be." Feel the energy of your desire flowing towards the candle and towards the person you want to recover.

Repeat for nine days: Repeat this process for nine consecutive days. Each day, light the candle and stick a pin in the next marked part. Be sure to extinguish the candle before going to bed and light it up the next day.

Concentration and faith: Throughout the ritual, maintain an attitude of concentration, faith, and conviction. Believe in the power of your words and actions to rekindle the connection with your loved one.

Recommendations:

- Clearly visualize the image of the person you want to recover and the connection you want to rekindle with them.
- Express your desires with sincerity and emotion.
- Maintain a positive attitude throughout the process.
- Be patient and trust in the power of the ritual.

Considerations:

It is important to keep in mind that this ritual is a tool that can help you recover your loved one, but its success depends largely on your own effort and commitment. True love is based on respect, communication, trust, and mutual support. If your intention is to manipulate or control the other person, this ritual will not give you the results you want.

Warning:

This ritual should not be used to harm or hurt anyone. True love is based on free will and mutual respect. If your intention is to harm or hurt the other person, this ritual will not give you the results you want.

Remember:

This ritual can be a tool to help you rekindle the connection with your loved one, but the real work is up to you. Reflect on your relationship and find ways to improve it. Open communication, mutual respect, and joint effort are keys to a healthy and lasting relationship.

Bring Back Your Lover:
A Ritual to Rekindle Love

Materials:

- A virgin parchment paper
- A needle
- A small amount of blood
- A red pen or feather
- A white candle
- A small plate

Preparation:

Choose the location: Perform the ritual in a quiet and private place where you can concentrate without interruptions.

Preparation of the parchment: With the needle, extract a small amount of blood from your ring finger. Blood symbolizes vitality and connection with your loved one.

Writing of the names: With the red pen or feather and the blood, write your names and the name of your loved one in a small circle in the center of the parchment. Clearly visualize the image of the person you want to recover and the connection you want to rekindle with them.

Drawing of circles: Surround the central circle with three other blood circles. These circles represent the protection and power of the ritual.

Folding and burying: Fold the parchment carefully and place it on a small plate. Light the white candle and place it next to the plate. Visualize how the flame of the candle illuminates your desire to rekindle the love with your loved one.

Prayer of love:

Recite the following prayer with faith and conviction:

(Prayer to Saint Cyprian)

Saint Cyprian, blessed among saints, I implore your favor. Make (name of loved one) feel that they need me near, that they cannot bear my absence and call me. And to be able to feel them, enjoy them and adore them once more.

Leave the ritual overnight: Leave the plate with the parchment, the candle, and the prayer next to your bed for the whole night. As you fall asleep, visualize the love you feel for your loved one and the desire to have them back in your life.

Recommendations:

- Visualize clearly the image of the person you want to recover and the connection you want to rekindle with them.
- Express your desires with sincerity and emotion.
- Maintain a positive attitude throughout the process.
- Be patient and trust in the power of the ritual.

Considerations:

It is important to keep in mind that this ritual is a tool that can help you recover your loved one, but its success depends largely on your own effort and commitment. True love is based on respect, communication, trust, and mutual support. If your intention is to manipulate or control the other person, this ritual will not give you the results you want.

Warning:

This ritual should not be used to harm or hurt anyone. True love is based on free will and mutual respect. If your intention is to harm or hurt the other person, this ritual will not give you the results you want.

Remember:

This ritual can be a tool to help you rekindle the connection with your loved one, but the real work is up to you. Reflect on your relationship and find ways to improve it. Open communication, mutual respect, and joint effort are keys to a healthy and lasting relationship.

ABUNDANCE

RITUALS

Rituals for Abundance and Good Luck: Attracting Prosperity to Your Home

The Elephant of Fortune: A Symbol of Abundance

In the world of Feng Shui, the elephant represents good luck, wisdom, and prosperity. It is believed that this noble animal attracts positive energy to your home and helps you achieve your financial goals.

To incorporate this symbol of abundance into your life, you can perform the following ritual:

Materials:

- Elephant figurine (with the trunk facing up)
- Bill of any denomination

Steps:

1. **Place the elephant figurine:** Place the elephant figurine near the front door of your home, with the trunk facing the entrance.

2. **Activate prosperity:** Roll up a bill of any denomination and secure it to the elephant's trunk. This symbolizes attracting financial abundance into your home.

3. **Intention and visualization:** Focus on your desires for prosperity and abundance. Visualize the elephant helping you achieve your financial goals and attracting positive opportunities.

Additional Tips:

- You can place the elephant on a side table or shelf near the entrance.
- Make sure the elephant figurine is in good condition and free of dust.
- Clean the elephant with a damp cloth regularly to maintain its positive energy.
- Combine this ritual with other Feng Shui principles to create a harmonious and prosperous environment in your home.

Remember that this ritual is a tool to complement your efforts and your positive attitude towards abundance. True prosperity is achieved through hard work, perseverance, and an open mind to opportunities.

More Abundance Rituals:

- **Abundance amulet:** Create an amulet with elements that represent prosperity to you, such as coins, gemstones, or symbols of abundance. Carry this amulet with you as a reminder of your goals and attract good luck on your path.

- **Positive affirmations:** Repeat positive affirmations related to abundance and prosperity. Statements like "I am a magnet for abundance" or "Prosperity flows to me naturally" can help you reprogram your subconscious mind and attract the energies you desire.

Remember that true magic lies within you. Cultivate a positive mindset, take concrete actions towards your goals, and use these rituals as tools to empower your path to abundance and prosperity.

Breath of Abundance:
A Cinnamon Ritual for Prosperity

Attracting prosperity and abundance into your life is a common desire, and many people turn to different methods to achieve it. A popular ritual that uses the power of cinnamon is the "Breath of Abundance."

What do you need?

- A handful of powdered cinnamon (not cinnamon sticks)
- Your firm and intentional voice

How to do it:

Choose the right time: Some recommend performing this ritual on the first Sunday of the month, during the day.

Take the cinnamon: Hold a handful of powdered cinnamon firmly in your right hand.

Go to the right place: Go to the front door of your home, office, or place where you want to attract financial abundance. Stand outside, facing inside.

Declare your intentions: With a clear and confident voice, say the following statement three times:

"When I blow this cinnamon, prosperity will come here. When I blow this cinnamon, abundance will come to stay. When I blow this cinnamon, abundance will live here."

Blow the cinnamon: Blow the powdered cinnamon forcefully, spreading the aroma inside the place.

Let the magic work: Do not sweep the floor for the first 24 hours. Some recommend keeping the cinnamon until the end of the month.

Additional tips:

- Visualize while performing the ritual: Imagine the cinnamon attracting positive energy and abundance to your home or business.
- Believe in the power of the ritual: Faith and conviction are key to making this type of practice work.
- Combine the ritual with concrete actions: Work hard, persevere in your goals, and make sound financial decisions to complement the power of the ritual.

Keep in mind:

- This ritual is not a substitute for hard work or sound financial decisions.
- It is important to have faith and believe in the power of attraction for the ritual to work.

- If you don't see immediate results, don't be discouraged. Keep practicing the ritual and focus on maintaining a positive and prosperous attitude.

Attracting abundance into your life is possible with the combination of concrete actions, a positive mindset, and the help of tools like this cinnamon ritual. Go ahead and try it and experience the power of attraction!

Energy Cleaning Rituals with Salt: Attracting Prosperity and Peace to Your Home

Salt is an ancient element with a deep spiritual and energetic meaning. In different cultures, it is attributed with the power to cleanse, protect, and attract positive energies.

Here is an energy cleaning ritual with salt, ideal to perform on the first Sunday of each month and attract prosperity and peace to your home:

Materials:

- Coarse or sea salt
- Water
- Transparent glass
- Precious crystals (optional)

- Pot with soil (optional)

Steps:

1. **Prepare the mixture:** In a transparent glass, mix coarse or sea salt with water until completely dissolved.

2. **Infuse positive energy (optional):** If you want to enhance the energy of the ritual, you can surround the glass with precious crystals for an hour while the mixture rests.

3. **Let it rest:** Allow the salt and water mixture to rest for an hour.

4. **Hand washing:** Once the resting time has passed, wash your hands with the salt and water mixture. While doing so, recite the following phrase with conviction:

"The salt is protective, and it will help me multiply my money and never be lacking in my home."

5. **Contact with the earth (optional):** It is recommended to wash your hands outdoors or over a pot of soil. In this way, salt and water come into contact with the earth, completing the energy cleaning cycle.

6. **Avoid soap and drying:** It is important not to wash your hands with soap after the ritual. You should also not rinse them or dry them with a towel or paper. Let the salt and water dry naturally on your hands.

Additional tips:

- You can repeat this ritual every first Sunday of the month to keep positive energy flowing in your home.
- Combine this ritual with other habits that promote prosperity and peace in your life, such as maintaining a positive attitude, practicing gratitude, and creating a harmonious environment in your home.
- Remember that this ritual is a complementary tool, and that true lasting changes are achieved with concrete actions and an open mind to opportunities.

Ritual variations:

- Some rituals suggest adding essential oils to the salt and water mixture, such as lavender or rosemary, to enhance their effects.
- You can also use the salt and water mixture to clean and energize different spaces in your home, such as spraying it in the corners or in the rooms where you feel stuck or with low energy.

Keep in mind:

- This ritual is not a substitute for hard work or good decisions in life.

- It is important to have faith and believe in the power of energy cleaning for the ritual to work.

- If you do not see immediate results, do not be discouraged. Keep practicing the ritual and focus on maintaining a positive and prosperous attitude.

Green Lotion for Prosperity:
Attract Abundance and Financial Strengthening

In the world of magic and popular traditions, the Green Lotion to Attract Money is presented as a simple but powerful ritual to attract abundance, prosperity, and strengthen your financial situation. Here are the steps to follow to perform this spell:

Materials:

- 1 liter of green fruit lotion
- 1 silver coin
- 1 new plain glass
- Water

Preparation:

- **Lunar phase:** Choose a night of the waxing moon to perform the ritual, as this phase is associated with growth and prosperity.

- **Glass preparation:** Fill the new plain glass with three-quarters full of water.

- **Coin placement:** Place the silver coin in the glass, making sure it is completely submerged in the water.

- **Lotion addition:** Fill the glass with the green fruit lotion until it is completely full.

- **Glass placement:** Place the glass in a visible place within your business or home, preferably on an altar or space dedicated to prosperity.

- **Natural evaporation:** Allow the liquid to evaporate on its own, without interfering with the process.

- **Ritual repetition:** Once the liquid has completely evaporated, carefully wash the glass and repeat the process with new ingredients.

Expected effects:

- **Attraction of well-paid work:** It is said that this spell favors the obtaining of job opportunities with good remuneration.

- **Business prosperity:** For business owners, it is associated with an increase in sales and a greater influx of customers.

- **Financial abundance:** In general, it is believed that Green Lotion attracts abundance and improves the financial situation in all aspects.

Additional recommendations:

- **Don Juan del Dinero prayer:** It is recommended to recite the Don Juan del Dinero prayer three times and any other prayer of abundance each time you repeat the ritual.
- **Rusty coins:** Observe the silver coin. If it begins to show rust or a white powder, it is considered that it has absorbed envy and should be replaced with a new one.
- **Faith and conviction:** Remember that the key to success in any ritual lies in the faith and conviction you have in its power. Maintain a positive attitude and focus on attracting prosperity into your life.

Keep in mind:

- **Complement, not substitute:** This ritual is a complementary tool to attract abundance, but it does not replace hard work, perseverance, and sound financial decisions.
- **Responsibility and ethics:** It is important to use this spell responsibly and ethically, always with the aim of improving your financial situation in an honest and fair way.

- **Respect and beliefs:** Respect the beliefs of others and avoid performing this ritual with negative or harmful intentions for other people.

Attracting prosperity and abundance into your life is possible with the combination of concrete actions, a positive mindset, and the help of tools like Green Lotion to Attract Money. Go ahead and try it and experience the power of attraction in your financial life!

Prayer to Don Juan of Money

I (your name) invoke Don Juan of Money, his benevolent spirit to be my support and help, that he may protect my body and soul. I ask that he may provide me with abundant wealth and happiness, and that every project I undertake, may have his blessing so that I may triumph and enjoy success. I ask with all my heart that you free me from this poverty, from this economic hardship and scarcity that I am suffering, grant me from now on too much abundance and happiness, and illuminate me with that star of good luck every day so that success may accompany me in every business that I undertake during my life. I take refuge in Don Juan of Money; I beg you please do not forget me and do not abandon me your faithful servant.

Red Egg to Boost Sales:
Attract Prosperity and Eliminate Negative Energies

In the realm of popular traditions and beliefs, the Red Egg to Increase Sales is presented as a simple but effective ritual to attract prosperity, eliminate bad vibrations, and boost sales in your business. Here are the steps to follow to perform this spell:

Materials:

- 1 egg
- Red paint
- Brush

Preparation:

- **Lunar phase:** Choose the first day of the full moon each month to perform the ritual, as this phase is associated with growth, fullness, and abundance.
- **Egg preparation:** Paint the egg a uniform red color using the brush. Make sure to cover the entire surface of the egg.
- **Egg placement:** Place the red egg in a safe place inside your business or home, preferably on an altar or space dedicated to prosperity.

- **Energy charging:** Leave the red egg in place throughout the lunar cycle, allowing it to absorb the positive energy of the full moon.

- **Egg renewal:** When the next full moon arrives, repeat the process: paint a new egg red, place it in the same spot, and discard the previous egg.

Expected effects:

- **Increased sales:** It is believed that this spell favors an increase in sales and customer influx in your business.

- **Prosperity and abundance:** The Red Egg is also associated with attracting general prosperity and abundance in your financial life.

- **Elimination of bad vibrations:** It is said that this ritual helps to cleanse and eliminate negative energies present in your business or home, creating a more harmonious environment for success.

Additional recommendations:

- **Money and abundance prayer:** During the process of painting the red egg and placing it in its place, you can recite a money and abundance prayer three times to enhance its effects.

- **Positive visualization:** While performing the ritual, maintain a positive attitude and visualize your business prospering, sales increasing, and abundance flowing towards you.

- **Faith and conviction:** Remember that the key to success in any ritual lies in the faith and conviction you have in its power. Maintain an open mind and focus on attracting prosperity into your life.

Keep in mind:

- **Complement, not substitute:** This ritual is a complementary tool to attract abundance, but it does not replace hard work, perseverance, and effective business strategies.
- **Responsibility and ethics:** It is important to use this spell responsibly and ethically, always with the aim of improving your financial situation in an honest and fair way.
- **Respect and beliefs:** Respect the beliefs of others and avoid performing this ritual with negative or harmful intentions for other people.

Attracting prosperity, abundance, and success in your business is possible with the combination of concrete actions, a positive mindset, and the help of tools like the Red Egg to Increase Sales. Go ahead and try it and experience the power of attraction in your financial life!

Mustard for Fortune:
Attract Luck and Abundance with a Simple Ritual

In the world of popular beliefs and home magic, Mustard for Fortune is presented as a simple but effective ritual to attract luck, abundance, and prosperity into your life. Here are the steps to follow to perform this spell:

Materials:

- 1 kilogram of mustard seeds
- 1 small copper pot

Preparation:

- **Lunar phase:** Choose a night of the waxing moon to perform the ritual, as this phase is associated with growth, abundance, and renewal.
- **Mustard preparation:** Place the mustard seeds inside the small copper pot.
- **Pot placement:** Place the pot with the mustard in a visible place inside your home or business, preferably on an altar or space dedicated to fortune.
- **Energy charging:** Leave the pot with mustard throughout the lunar cycle, allowing it to absorb the positive energy of the waxing moon.

- **Mustard renewal:** When the next waxing moon arrives, repeat the process: fill a new copper pot with mustard seeds, place it in the same spot, and discard the mustard and the previous pot.

Using the mustard:

- **To attract luck:** Take a pinch of mustard seeds with your fingers and rub them on an object that has special meaning to you, such as an amulet, a piece of jewelry, or a work tool. Visualize how luck and abundance are associated with that object.
- **To enhance rituals:** You can use mustard seeds as an additional ingredient in other luck and abundance rituals. For example, you can add them to herbal baths or prosperity candles.

Additional recommendations:

- **Fortune prayer:** During the process of preparing the mustard and placing it in its place, you can recite a fortune prayer to enhance its effects. You can find various fortune prayers in prayer books or on the internet.
- **Positive visualization:** While performing the ritual, maintain a positive attitude and visualize how luck accompanies you in all your projects and endeavors.

- **Faith and conviction:** Remember that the key to success in any ritual lies in the faith and conviction you have in its power. Maintain an open mind and focus on attracting fortune into your life.

Keep in mind:

- **Complement, not substitute:** This ritual is a complementary tool to attract abundance, but it does not replace hard work, perseverance, and sound decision-making.
- **Responsibility and ethics:** It is important to use this spell responsibly and ethically, always with the aim of improving your life in an honest and fair way.
- **Respect and beliefs:** Respect the beliefs of others and avoid performing this ritual with negative or harmful intentions for other people.

Attracting luck, abundance, and prosperity into your life is possible with the combination of concrete actions, a positive mindset, and the help of tools like Mustard for Fortune. Go ahead and try it and experience the power of attraction in your life!

Money Bills for Abundance:
Attract Prosperity with a Simple Ritual

In the world of rituals and popular beliefs, Money Bills for Abundance are presented as a simple but effective spell to attract financial prosperity and abundance into your life. Here are the steps to follow to perform this ritual:

Materials:

- A pack of Monopoly money
- 50 grams of sandalwood essence
- A dropper

Preparation:

- **Lunar phase:** Choose a night of the waxing moon to perform the ritual, as this phase is associated with growth, renewal, and abundance.
- **Bill preparation:** Carefully anoint each bill in the Monopoly pack with a few drops of sandalwood essence using the dropper.
- **Bill placement:**
  - **For women:** Place the sandalwood-anointed bills under your mattress.
  - **For men:** You can carry the anointed bills with you in your wallet.

Ritual activation:

- **Visualization:** While anointing the bills with sandalwood, visualize them turning into real money, attracting prosperity and financial abundance to you.
- **Energy magnetic field:** With the energy of the waxing moon and visualization, a magnetic field of energy is created to attract money.

Reciting the prayer:

It is recommended to recite the Don Juan of Money prayer three times a day, touching the sandalwood-anointed bills, to enhance the effects of the ritual.

Additional recommendations:

- **Faith and conviction:** Remember that the key to success in any ritual lies in the faith and conviction you have in its power. Maintain a positive mindset and focus on attracting abundance into your life.
- **Consistency:** Perform the ritual consistently throughout the lunar cycle for better results.
- **Gratitude:** Express gratitude for the blessings you have already received and for those you wish to attract in the future.

Keep in mind:

- **Complement, not substitute:** This ritual is a complementary tool to attract abundance, but it does not replace hard work, perseverance, and sound financial decisions.

- **Responsibility and ethics:** It is important to use this spell responsibly and ethically, always with the aim of improving your financial situation in an honest and fair way.

- **Respect and beliefs:** Respect the beliefs of others and avoid performing this ritual with negative or harmful intentions for other people.

Attracting luck, abundance, and prosperity into your life is possible with the combination of concrete actions, a positive mindset, and the help of tools like Money Bills for Abundance. Go ahead and try it and experience the power of attraction in your financial life!

Sugar Bill Ritual to Attract Prosperity and Abundance

In the realm of rituals and popular beliefs, the Sugar Bill Ritual is presented as a simple but effective practice to attract financial prosperity and abundance into your life. Here are the steps to follow to perform this ritual:

Ideal time:

It is recommended to carry out this ritual during the full moon night, as this lunar phase is associated with fullness, the manifestation of desires, and receptive energy, creating a favorable environment for attracting abundance.

Materials:

- A glass jar with a lid
- A bill of any value (preferably one you don't use frequently)
- Sugar

Preparation:

- **Energy cleansing:** Begin by energetically cleansing the inside and outside of the glass jar. You can use a palo santo, incense, or smudging stick to remove any negative energy and prepare the container for the ritual.

- **Bill placement:** Carefully roll up the money bill and place it in the center of the clean glass jar.

- **Filling with sugar:** Pour sugar into the jar until it is completely full, completely covering the rolled-up bill. Sugar symbolizes the abundance and sweetness you want to attract into your financial life.

- **Exposure to moonlight:** Close the jar tightly with its lid and place it outdoors where it can receive direct moonlight for three consecutive nights. The full moon's energy will permeate the bill and sugar, enhancing the effects of the ritual.

- **Bill retrieval:** At the end of the third night, remove the jar from outside and carefully open the lid. Take the rolled-up bill out of the sugar and keep it in your wallet as a charm of good fortune and prosperity.

Additional recommendations:

- **Visualization and faith:** During the preparation process and while the jar is exposed to the full moon, it is important to maintain a positive attitude and visualize how abundance and prosperity flow towards you. Faith and conviction in the ritual are keys to its success.

- **Gratitude:** Express gratitude for the financial blessings you have already received and for those you wish to attract in the future. Cultivate an abundance and appreciation mindset.

- **Bill use:** You can use the bill as part of your daily transactions but avoid spending it immediately. Consider it a symbol of the abundance you are attracting into your life.

Keep in mind:

- **Complement, not substitute:** This ritual is a complementary tool to attract abundance, but it does not replace hard work, perseverance, and sound financial decisions.
- **Responsibility and ethics:** It is important to use this spell responsibly and ethically, always with the aim of improving your financial situation in an honest and fair way.
- **Respect and beliefs:** Respect the beliefs of others and avoid performing this ritual with negative or harmful intentions for other people.

Attracting luck, abundance, and prosperity into your life is possible with the combination of concrete actions, a positive mindset, and the help of tools like the Sugar Bill Ritual. Go ahead and try it and experience the power of attraction in your financial life!

Attract Abundance with the Power of Feng Shui and Purple Candles

In the fascinating world of Feng Shui, candles not only illuminate spaces but can also be powerful tools to attract positive energies and manifest our desires. In particular, purple candles are known for their ability to stimulate and increase financial abundance.

Here is a simple ritual to attract abundance into your life using a purple candle:

Materials:

- A purple candle
- An incense burner or smudging stick (optional)
- Paper and pencil
- A fireproof container (to place the candle)

Preparation:

- **Choose an appropriate time and place:** Find a quiet time when you can concentrate without interruption. Choose a place in your home that brings you peace and harmony, such as your bedroom or a meditation space.
- **Cleanse the space:** Light an incense burner or smudging stick to cleanse the environment of negative energies and

create an atmosphere conducive to the ritual. You can use aromas like sandalwood, lavender, or palo santo.

- **Define your intentions:** On a piece of paper, write a list of your desires related to abundance. Be specific and detailed about what you want to attract into your financial life.

- **Light the purple candle:** Place the purple candle in a fireproof container and light it carefully. Observe the flame and visualize how its light illuminates your desires and fills them with positive energy.

- **Recite an affirmation:** While the candle burns, recite a positive affirmation related to abundance out loud. For example, you could say: "I am a magnet for prosperity. Money flows to me easily and abundantly."

- **Give thanks and visualize:** Express gratitude for the financial blessings you have already received in your life. Then, close your eyes and visualize how you achieve your financial goals and enjoy a prosperous and abundant life.

- **Extinguish the candle with gratitude:** When the candle has burned down completely or when you feel that you have completed the ritual, carefully extinguish it. Thank again for the opportunity to perform this ritual and for the positive energy you have attracted.

Additional recommendations:

- **Repeat the ritual:** You can repeat this ritual regularly, for example, once a week or during the full moon, to enhance its effects.

- **Combine with other Feng Shui principles:** For better results, combine this ritual with other Feng Shui practices for abundance, such as keeping your home tidy and decorated with elements that represent prosperity.

- **Maintain a positive attitude:** Remember that the key to success in any ritual lies in the faith and conviction you have in its power. Maintain a positive attitude and focus on attracting abundance into your life.

Keep in mind:

- **Complement, not substitute:** This ritual is a complementary tool to attract abundance, but it does not replace hard work, making sound financial decisions, and managing your resources responsibly.

- **Responsibility and ethics:** It is important to use this ritual responsibly and ethically, always with the aim of improving your financial situation in an honest and fair way.

- **Respect and beliefs:** Respect the beliefs of others and avoid performing this ritual with negative or harmful intentions for other people.

Attracting prosperity and abundance into your life is possible with the combination of concrete actions, a positive mindset, responsible financial management, and the help of tools like the purple candle ritual and Feng Shui principles. Go ahead and try it and experience the power of attraction on your path to abundance!

PURIFICATION

RITUALS

Spells to Ward Off Black Magic and Bad Influences: Invoking Saint Clare for Peace and Harmony

In the world of popular traditions and beliefs, there are various spells and rituals to protect oneself from black magic, bad influences, and attract peace and harmony into your life. Here is a spell dedicated to Saint Clare, known for her power to ward off negative energies and provide protection.

Materials:

- 1 egg
- 1 new glass
- Water
- 9 white candles
- Prayer to Saint Clare

Preparation:

- **Fill the glass with water:** Pour clean water into the new glass until it is half full.
- **Place the egg:** Carefully place the egg in the water, making sure it is completely submerged.
- **Invoke Saint Clare:** Light one of the white candles and recite the prayer to Saint Clare three times with devotion. Ask for her intervention to bring peace and harmony into your life, driving away anything bad that may affect you.

- **Light the remaining candles:** Light one white candle per day for the next nine days. Each time you light a candle, recite the prayer to Saint Clare and renew your request for protection and harmony.

- **Disposal of the ritual:** At the end of the nine days, take the glass of water and egg to a park or a place away from your home. Pour the water on the ground and smash the egg against the earth with force. Visualize how with this act all the bad things that plagued you are broken and disappear.

- **Final request:** Once you have disposed of the water and the egg, light another white candle and recite the prayer to Saint Clare one last time. Thank her for her protection and reiterate your desire to live in peace and harmony.

Additional recommendations:

- **Faith and conviction:** The key to success in any ritual lies in the faith and conviction you have in its power. Maintain a positive attitude and trust in Saint Clare's protection.

- **Visualization:** During the ritual, visualize how the light of the candles and the energy of the prayer envelop your home and your life, driving away any negative influence and creating a harmonious environment.

- **Energy cleansing:** You can complement this ritual with energy cleansings in your home using incense, smudging sticks, or aromatic herbs such as sage or rosemary.

- **Personalized prayer:** If you wish, you can adapt the prayer to Saint Clare or create your own that expresses your personal request for protection and harmony.

Keep in mind:

- **Complement, not substitute:** This ritual is a complementary tool for protection and harmony, but it does not replace seeking professional help in cases of situations that require specialized psychological or spiritual attention.
- **Responsibility and ethics:** It is important to use this spell responsibly and ethically, always with the aim of protecting yourself and others from any negative energy.
- **Respect and beliefs:** Respect the beliefs of others and avoid performing this ritual with negative or harmful intentions for other people.

Attracting peace, harmony, and warding off bad influences from your life is possible with the combination of concrete actions, a positive mindset, the energy protection of your home, and the help of tools like the spell invoked to Saint Clare. Go ahead and try it and experience the power of faith and positive energy on your path to a more peaceful and harmonious life!

Nullify an Evil Spell and Return It to Its Origin with the Traditional Revocation of Saint Michael the Archangel

In the realm of popular beliefs and spiritual protection, the Traditional Revocation of Saint Michael the Archangel is presented as a powerful ritual to nullify an evil spell, break its negative influence, and return it to whoever sent it. Here are the steps to follow to perform this ritual:

Materials:

- 1 new glass
- Clean water
- 1 small coffee saucer
- 1 Saint Michael the Archangel candle
- Prayer to Saint Michael the Archangel

Preparation:

- **Fill the glass with water:** Pour clean water into the new glass until it is about three-quarters full.
- **Cover the glass:** Place the small coffee saucer upside down on the glass, completely covering it. Make sure the water does not spill.
- **Invert the glass:** Carefully invert the glass and saucer together, leaving the glass upside down on the saucer.

The candle will be in an inverted position, with the wick facing upwards.

- **Light the candle:** Light the wick of the Saint Michael the Archangel candle and recite the prayer to Saint Michael the Archangel three times with devotion. Ask for his intervention to reverse the course of the evil spell and return it to whoever sent it, just as the glass and candle have been inverted.

- **Request and visualization:** Visualize how the energy of the candle and the prayer of Saint Michael the Archangel surround your home and your being, breaking any negative influence and returning the spell to its origin.

- **Repetition of the ritual:** If you do not feel a significant improvement after the first three times, you can repeat the ritual for nine consecutive Tuesdays.

Additional recommendations:

- **Faith and conviction:** The key to success in any ritual lies in the faith and conviction you have in its power. Maintain a positive attitude and trust in the protection of Saint Michael the Archangel.

- **Energy cleansing:** You can complement this ritual with energy cleansings in your home using incense, smudging sticks, or aromatic herbs such as sage or rosemary.

- **Personalized prayer:** If you wish, you can adapt the prayer to Saint Michael the Archangel or create your own that expresses your personal request for the spell to be nullified and protection.

Keep in mind:

- **Complement, not substitute:** This ritual is a complementary tool for spiritual protection, but it does not replace seeking professional help in cases of situations that require specialized psychological or spiritual attention.
- **Responsibility and ethics:** It is important to use this spell responsibly and ethically, always with the aim of protecting yourself and others from any negative energy.
- **Respect and beliefs:** Respect the beliefs of others and avoid performing this ritual with negative or harmful intentions for other people.

Nullifying an evil spell, regaining your peace, and returning negative energy to its origin is possible with the combination of concrete actions, a positive mindset, the energy protection of your home, and the help of tools like the Traditional Revocation of Saint Michael the Archangel. Go ahead and try it and experience the power of faith and positive energy on your path to a more peaceful and protected life!

Free Yourself from All Evil: Protection Ritual with White Flowers and Siete Machos Lotion

In the realm of popular beliefs and the search for spiritual protection, this ritual presents a powerful tool to cleanse oneself of negative energies, break spiritual chains, and free oneself from all evil, especially that caused by visible or invisible enemies. Here are the steps to follow to perform this ritual:

Materials:

- 12 white flowers (roses, jasmine, lilies, etc.)
- Siete Machos Lotion (found online)
- 1 transparent plastic bag

Preparation:

- **Choose the right time:** You can start this ritual any day of the week. Find a quiet time when you can concentrate without interruption and connect with your spirituality.
- **Prepare the flowers:** Soak the 12 white flowers in the Siete Machos lotion, making sure they are well moistened.
- **Start the cleansing:** Starting from the head, cleanse your body with the flowers moistened in Siete Machos lotion. Make smooth, slow movements, covering all parts of your body, from head to toe.

- **Recite the prayer with fervor:** While performing the cleansing, recite the prayer with devotion and faith. Focus on each word and feel the protective energy enveloping you.

Prayer:

Protective spirit, protect me from my enemies, visible or invisible. I beg you to break the chains of misonic larvae that bite from above, from the middle and from below; so that my soul and my matter are freed from the negative effluvia of my enemies. You, who are powerful and who are the creator of all that is visible and invisible, of all that exists, I come to you with all my faith, so that you may free me from all evil, especially from... (say the problem that afflicts you). Thank you Father that you have heard me and by your kindness I am left healthy, clean and in peace. Amen.

Finish the ritual: Once you have cleansed your entire body and recited the entire prayer, place the flowers moistened in Siete Machos lotion inside the plastic bag.

Discard the bag: Close the bag tightly and take it to a place away from your home, such as a crossroads or a river. Leave the bag there and visualize how all the negative energies are moving away from you.

Additional recommendations:

- **Faith and conviction:** The key to success in any ritual lies in the faith and conviction you have in its power. Maintain a positive attitude and trust in the spiritual protection you are requesting.

- **Visualization:** During the ritual, visualize how the white light of the flowers and the energy of the prayer envelop your body and home, creating a protective shield against any negative energy.

- **Energy cleansing:** You can complement this ritual with energy cleansings in your home using incense, smudging sticks, or aromatic herbs such as sage or rosemary.

- **Repetition:** If you feel you need it, you can repeat this ritual regularly, for example, once a month or when you feel that your energy is being affected by negative energies.

Keep in mind:

- **Complement, not substitute:** This ritual is a complementary tool for spiritual protection, but it does not replace seeking professional help in cases of situations that require specialized psychological or spiritual attention.

- **Responsibility and ethics:** It is important to use this ritual responsibly and ethically, always with the aim of protecting yourself and others from any negative energy.
- **Respect and beliefs:** Respect the beliefs of others and avoid performing this ritual with negative or harmful intentions for other people.

Freeing yourself from negative energies and spiritual chains and achieving protection and peace of mind is possible with the combination of concrete actions, a positive mindset, spiritual cleansing of your home, and the help of tools like the Protection Ritual with White Flowers and Siete Machos Lotion. Go ahead and try it and experience the power of faith, positive energy, and spiritual protection on your path to a more harmonious and protected life.

Purify and Free Yourself from All Evil with the Blessing of Water

In the realm of popular beliefs and the search for spiritual purification, this ritual presents a powerful tool to cleanse your body, mind, and spirit of negative energies, break spiritual chains, and free yourself from all evil, especially that caused by visible or invisible enemies. Here are the steps to follow to perform this ritual:

Materials:

- A container with clean water
- Sea salt
- White flower petals (roses, jasmine, lilies, etc.)
- Incense or smudge stick (optional)
- White candle (optional)
- Protection prayer (optional)

Preparation:

- **Choose the right time:** Find a quiet time when you can concentrate without interruption and connect with your spirituality. You can perform this ritual any day of the week, but it is recommended to do it on the waning moon to enhance the energy cleansing.

- **Prepare the water:** Fill the container with clean water until it is half full. Add a tablespoon of sea salt and stir gently to dissolve it. If you wish, you can also add white flower petals to give the water a pleasant aroma.

- **Light the incense or candle (optional):** If you want to create an environment more conducive to concentration and spiritual connection, you can light incense or a white candle.

- **Recite the protection prayer (optional):** If you have a personal protection prayer or one that makes you feel connected to your faith, you can recite it at this time.

Performing the ritual:

- **Stand in front of the container of water:** Stand barefoot in front of the container of water with a reverent attitude. You can place your hands on the container or at the sides of your body.

- **Close your eyes and breathe deeply:** Inhale and exhale calmly, connecting with your breath and focusing your attention on the present moment. Visualize how negative energy leaves your body and dissolves into the water.

- **Cleanse with the water:** Take some water in your hands and sprinkle it over your head, shoulders, chest, back, abdomen, legs, and feet. Repeat this action while reciting the following prayer or any other that makes you feel protected and connected to your faith:

Heavenly Father, I ask you to bless this water and fill it with your purifying light. May it, as I sprinkle it on my body, cleanse all the negative energies that afflict me, visible or invisible. Break the spiritual chains that bind me and free my soul and my matter from any curse or negative influence. Protect my body, mind and spirit from all evil and allow me to live in peace and harmony. Thank you for your infinite mercy and love.

- **Visualize the cleansing:** As you sprinkle the water on your body, visualize how the white light and purifying energy of the water penetrate every part of your being, eliminating any trace of negativity.

- **Express gratitude and seal the cleansing:** Once you have finished sprinkling yourself with the water, express gratitude for the blessing received and visualize how your body is enveloped in a protective shield of white light.

Disposal of the water:

- **If you used flowers:** Remove the flower petals from the water and discard the water in a place away from your home, such as a river or a crossroads.

- **If you did not use flowers:** You can pour the water directly down the sink or toilet, visualizing how the negative energy is moving away from your life.

Additional recommendations:

- **Faith and conviction:** The key to success in any ritual lies in the faith and conviction you have in its power. Maintain a positive attitude and trust in the protection you are requesting.

- **Visualization:** During the ritual, it is important that you focus on visualizing the cleansing and protection. Visualization is a powerful tool to enhance the effectiveness of the ritual.

- **Energy cleansing:** You can complement this ritual with energy cleansings in your home using incense, smudging sticks, or aromatic herbs such as sage or rosemary.

- **Repetition:** If you feel you need it, you can repeat this ritual regularly, for example, once a month or when you feel that your energy is being affected by negative energies.

Keep in mind:

- **Complement, not substitute:** This ritual is a complementary tool for spiritual protection, but it does not replace seeking professional help in cases of situations that require specialized psychological or spiritual attention.

- **Responsibility and ethics:** It is important to use this ritual responsibly and ethically, always with the aim of protecting yourself and others from any negative energy.
- **Respect and beliefs:** Respect the beliefs of others and avoid performing this ritual with negative or harmful intentions for other people.

Purifying yourself from negative energies and spiritual chains and achieving protection and peace of mind is possible with the combination of concrete actions, a positive mindset, spiritual cleansing of your home, and the help of tools like the Blessing of Water ritual. Go ahead

Neutralize Envy and Attract Positivity with the Gunpowder and Vinegar Ritual

In the realm of popular beliefs and the pursuit of well-being, the Gunpowder and Vinegar Ritual is presented as a tool to neutralize envy, attract positive energies, and protect your home or business. Here are the steps to follow to perform this ritual:

Materials:

- 3 tablespoons of gunpowder
- 3 tablespoons of white vinegar

- Water (enough to fill a mop bucket)
- Mop bucket
- Mop

Preparation:

- **Fill the bucket with water:** Pour clean water into the mop bucket until it is about half full.
- **Add the ingredients:** Add the 3 tablespoons of gunpowder and the 3 tablespoons of white vinegar to the water in the bucket. Stir well to completely dissolve the ingredients.
- **Recite the "House of Jerusalem" prayer (optional):** If you wish to enhance the ritual with a prayer of protection, you can recite the "House of Jerusalem" prayer while preparing the mixture.

Performing the ritual:

- **Mop your home or business:** Use the mop soaked in water, gunpowder, and vinegar mixture to mop your home or business as usual. Pay attention to corners, nooks, and places where negative energy may accumulate.
- **Visualize the neutralization of envy:** As you mop, visualize how the gunpowder and vinegar mixture absorbs and neutralizes any negative or envious energy that may be

present in the environment. Imagine your home or business filling with light and positivity.

- **Repeat the "House of Jerusalem" prayer (optional):** If you are reciting the prayer, continue to do so as you mop.

- **Rinse the mop:** Once you have finished mopping, rinse the mop thoroughly with clean water to remove any residue from the mixture.

- **Dispose of the water:** Pour the water from the bucket down the toilet or drain, visualizing how the negative energies are moving away from your home or business.

Additional recommendations:

- **Frequency:** You can perform this ritual once a week or more often if you feel that your home or business is being affected by negative energies or envy.

- **Combination with other rituals:** You can complement this ritual with other energy cleansing rituals, such as burning incense or smudging sticks, or using aromatic herbs such as sage or rosemary.

- **Positive attitude:** Maintain a positive attitude focused on neutralizing envy and attracting positive energies throughout the ritual.

Keep in mind:

- **Complement, not substitute:** This ritual is a complementary tool for energy cleansing and protection, but it does not replace seeking professional help in cases of situations that require specialized psychological or spiritual attention.
- **Responsibility and ethics:** It is important to use this ritual responsibly and ethically, always with the aim of protecting yourself and others from any negative energy.
- **Respect and beliefs:** Respect the beliefs of others and avoid performing this ritual with negative or harmful intentions for other people.

Neutralizing envy and attracting positive energy into your home or business is possible with the combination of concrete actions, a positive mindset, energy cleansing, and the help of tools like the Gunpowder and Vinegar Ritual. Go ahead and try it and experience the power of positive energy and spiritual protection in your environment!

MORE

RITUALS

Joy and Connection Ritual: Attracting Friendship, Creativity, and Renewal

Purpose: This ritual aims to attract joy, friendship, creativity, brilliant ideas, and overall renewal into your life. It is performed near the time when the Sun enters the sign of Aquarius, harnessing the energy of this sign to enhance its effects.

Materials:

- Clear quartz crystal
- Blue soap
- Water
- Sea salt
- Glass
- Aluminum foil
- Tarot card of the Star (Arcanum 17)

Preparation:

1. **Purify the quartz:** Wash the clear quartz crystal with blue soap to remove any negative energy.
2. **Charge the quartz:** In a glass, combine water and sea salt. Place the clear quartz crystal in the glass and let it rest under the moonlight overnight.

3. **Empower with Aquarius energy:** Wrap the glass with aluminum foil without covering it. Aluminum represents the metal of Uranus, the ruling planet of Aquarius, and will help boost the ritual's energy.

4. **Meditation with The Star:** On the morning of January 21st, at 5:30 am, perform a meditation with the Tarot card of the Star (Arcanum 17), the Aquarius card. Observe the card carefully for five minutes, connecting with its energy of joy, hope, and renewal.

5. **Activate the quartz:** Remove the quartz from the water and hold it between your hands. Repeat its name four times with intention and visualize it filling you with positive energy and attracting good things into your life.

6. **Store the quartz:** Wrap the quartz in aluminum foil and keep it on a bedside table all year round. Its energy will be with you constantly, attracting what you desire.

7. **Nurture connection:** During the day or night, invite your best friend to lunch, dinner, or a movie outing. Strengthening existing relationships is an important step in attracting new friendships and improving your social life.

Remember:

- This ritual is a tool to complement your own efforts and actions. It is not an instant magical formula.
- The key to success lies in your positive attitude, openness to new experiences, and willingness to connect with others.
- Perform this ritual with faith and enthusiasm and open your heart to the possibilities that life offers you.

Additional tips:

- You can add other elements to the ritual that represent joy, friendship, and renewal to you, such as flowers, candles, or relaxing music.
- If you don't have a clear quartz crystal, you can use another type of stone that attracts you and has special meaning to you.
- You can adapt the ritual to your own beliefs and preferences. The important thing is that you feel comfortable and connected to the energy you want to attract.
- May this ritual bring you joy, friendship, creativity, and a life full of possibilities!

Ritual to Awaken Intuition and Personal Magnetism

Objective: To awaken intuition, the sixth sense, and increase personal magnetism to attract others.

Ideal Moment: Under the influence of Pisces, when the energy favors intuition and sensitivity.

Date: February 18th

Time: 11:00 PM

Materials:

- Tarot cards: The Sun (arcanum 19) and the Moon (arcanum 18)
- Amethyst stone
- Blue soap
- Water
- Sea salt
- Tin
- Glass

Preparation:

1. **Meditation with the cards:** At 11:00 PM on February 18th, meditate with the Tarot cards The Sun (arcanum 19) and the Moon (arcanum 18). Focus on the energy of these cards, which represent intuition, receptivity, and connection to the inner world.

2. **Purify the amethyst:** Wash the amethyst stone with blue soap to remove any negative energy and prepare it for the ritual.

3. **Charge the amethyst:** In a glass, combine water and sea salt. Place the purified amethyst in the glass and let it rest under the moonlight overnight.

4. **Empower with tin:** Wrap the glass with tin, rolling it around the glass. Tin is a conductive metal that will help enhance the ritual's energy and attract personal magnetism.

5. **Activate the amethyst:** The next day, remove the amethyst from the water and hold it between your hands. Visualize how the energy of intuition and personal magnetism intensifies in the stone.

6. **Create your talisman:** Wrap the amethyst with the tin you used to surround the glass. This will be your personal talisman to enhance your intuition and magnetism.

7. **Carry your talisman with you:** Whenever you wish, carry your amethyst talisman wrapped in tin with you. Its energy

will accompany you, awakening your intuition and attracting others towards you.

Additional tips:

- You can add other elements to the ritual that represent intuition and personal magnetism to you, such as blue or violet candles, lavender incense, or sandalwood or jasmine essential oils.

- If you don't have tin, you can use another conductive metal like copper or silver.

- You can adapt the ritual to your own beliefs and preferences. The important thing is that you feel comfortable and connected to the energy you want to attract.

- May this ritual help you awaken your intuition, increase your personal magnetism, and attract positive people into your life!

Ritual for Abundance, Sensuality, and Energetic Connection

Objective: To attract prosperity, good business, increase sensuality, and connect with the energy of abundance and pleasure.

Ideal Moment: Night of April 19th, taking advantage of the energy of the waxing moon to enhance the effects of the ritual.

Materials:

- Aguardiente (a small amount)
- Rose petals
- Honey (one tablespoon)
- Rochela salt (or fig salt if not found)
- Rose essence
- Tarot card The Hierophant (arcanum 5)
- Tarot card The Empress (arcanum 3)

Preparation:

1. **Bath of prosperity and sensuality:** On the night of April 19th, prepare a special bath. Fill a tub with warm water and add:
   - A splash of aguardiente

- Rose petals to attract love and sensuality
- A tablespoon of honey to attract abundance and sweetness
- Rochela salt (or fig salt) for energy cleansing and prosperity
- A few drops of rose essence to enhance sensuality and connection

2. **Immersion in energy:** Immerse yourself in the bath, letting the water impregnate your body with the energies of prosperity, sensuality, and connection. Relax, breathe deeply, and visualize how abundance and pleasure flow towards you.

3. **Restorative sleep:** After the bath, go to bed and allow the energies of the ritual to integrate into your being overnight.

4. **Morning meditation:** At 5:45 am the next day, meditate with the Tarot cards The Hierophant (arcanum 5) and The Empress (arcanum 3). These cards represent material and spiritual abundance, connection with the creative feminine energy, and the manifestation of your desires.

5. **Gratitude and action:** Give thanks for the abundance that already exists in your life and for what is to come. Visualize your goals of prosperity and sensuality with clarity and determination. Take action to turn your desires into reality.

Additional tips:

- You can add relaxing music, candles, or incense during the bath to create an atmosphere conducive to meditation and energetic connection.
- If you don't have fresh rose petals, you can use dried petals or rose essence.
- You can repeat this ritual every month to keep the energy of abundance and sensuality flowing in your life.
- May this ritual help you attract prosperity, sensuality, and connect with the energy of pleasure and abundance in all aspects of your life!

Ritual for Eloquence, Connection, and Love: Communicating Successfully

Objective: To improve communication, the ability to express oneself fluently, connect with others, and attract love.

Ideal Moment: Night of May 20th, taking advantage of the energy of the waxing moon to enhance the effects of the ritual.

Materials:

- Rutilated quartz stone
- Blue soap

- Water

- Sea salt

- Glass

- Thermometer

- Tarot card The Lovers (arcanum 6)

Preparation:

1. **Purify the quartz:** Wash the rutilated quartz stone with blue soap to remove any negative energy and prepare it for the ritual.

2. **Charge the quartz:** In a glass, combine water, sea salt, and the rutilated quartz. Also place a thermometer in the glass, as the mercury it contains represents the planet Mercury, ruler of Gemini and associated with communication. Leave the glass outside under the moonlight overnight.

3. **Meditation with The Lovers:** The next morning, meditate with the Tarot card The Lovers (arcanum 6). This card represents effective communication, the ability to connect with others, and the search for balance in relationships.

4. **Activate the quartz:** Remove the quartz from the water and hold it between your hands. Repeat its name six times with intention and visualize how it fills you with positive energy and improves your ability to communicate fluently and clearly.

5. **Place the elements:** Keep the thermometer on your bedside table, symbolizing connection and fluidity in communication. Place the rutilated quartz on or next to a television, as a decoration, so that it radiates its energy into your surroundings.

6. **Nurture connection:** Make a phone call to someone to say hello and strengthen your relationships. Start a flowing conversation, expressing yourself confidently and connecting with the other person.

Additional tips:

- You can add other elements to the ritual that represent communication, connection, and love to you, such as blue or green candles, lavender incense, or peppermint or rosemary essential oils.

- If you don't have rutilated quartz, you can use another stone that attracts you and has special meaning to you.

- You can adapt the ritual to your own beliefs and preferences. The important thing is that you feel comfortable and connected to the energy you want to attract.

- May this ritual help you improve your communication, connect with others effectively, and attract love into your life!

Summer Solstice Purification and Renewal Ritual

Objective: To harness the energy of the summer solstice and the feast of Saint John the Baptist to perform a purifying bath that releases guilt, traumas, fears, and dense energies, favoring spiritual elevation and personal renewal.

Ideal Moment: Night of June 20th, coinciding with the summer solstice and the celebration of Saint John the Baptist.

Materials:

- Tub
- White flowers (lilies, chrysanthemums, white roses)
- Peppermint essence
- White wine
- White candle
- Tarot card The Chariot (arcanum 7)

Preparation:

1. **Preparing the bath:** In a tub, prepare the purifying bath. Add white flowers to symbolize purity and renewal. Incorporate peppermint essence to enhance energy cleansing and freshness. Add a splash of white wine as a symbol of transformation and transmutation.

2.   **Lighting the flame:** Light a white candle at the base of the tub and let it burn throughout the night. Its light represents clarity, peace, and protection.

3.   **Meditation with The Chariot:** Before bed, meditate with the Tarot card The Chariot (arcanum 7). This card represents progress, overcoming obstacles, and connection with the higher self. Visualize how you free yourself from negative burdens and rise to a state of peace and well-being.

4.   **Purifying bath:** The next day, take the purifying bath with the water from the tub. Start with your head, pouring the water over your forehead like a symbolic baptism. Allow the water to flow all over your body, carrying away negative energies and making space for renewal.

Meaning and benefits:

This ritual symbolizes a new beginning, an opportunity to leave behind what limits you and embrace light and transformation.

The bath with white flowers, peppermint, and white wine cleanses your energy aura, freeing you from negative burdens and attracting positive energies.

Meditation with The Chariot connects you with your inner self and propels you forward towards your goals with determination and confidence.

This ritual helps you regain your inner peace, your emotional balance, and your connection with the spiritual.

Additional tips:

- You can add relaxing music or nature sounds during the bath to create an atmosphere conducive to meditation and renewal.
- You can repeat this ritual whenever you feel the need to purify and renew yourself energetically.
- Remember that this ritual is a tool complementary to your own personal effort to achieve well-being and fulfillment.
- May this ritual help you free yourself from what limits you, connect with your higher self, and begin a new stage full of light and renewal!

Ritual for Success, Fame, and Leadership: Shine with Your Own Light

Objective: To attract success, fame, leadership, the attention of others, and love, enhancing your charisma and personal magnetism.

Ideal Moment: Night of July 22nd, taking advantage of the energy of the Sun in Leo to enhance the effects of the ritual.

Materials:

- Tub
- Red wine (a small amount)
- Red rose petals
- Ground cinnamon
- Rochela salt (or fig salt if not found)
- Rose essence
- Sandalwood incense
- Tarot card The Strength (arcanum 8)
- Tarot card The Sun (arcanum 19)

Preparation:

1. **Power and magnetism bath:** On the night of July 22nd, prepare a special bath. Fill a tub with warm water and add:

   o   A splash of red wine to enhance passion and vital energy

- o   Red rose petals to attract love, sensuality, and personal magnetism

- o   Ground cinnamon to stimulate the mind, clarity, and success

- o   Rochela salt (or fig salt) for energy cleansing and protection

- o   A few drops of rose essence to intensify the aroma and emotional connection

2. **Activation with incense:** Light sandalwood incense, an aroma associated with prosperity, spirituality, and connection with the inner self. Let the smoke permeate the environment while you bathe.

3. **Immersion in energy:** Immerse yourself in the bath, letting the water and ingredients impregnate your body with the energies of success, fame, leadership, and personal magnetism. Visualize how you become the best version of yourself, attracting the attention, recognition, and love you desire.

4. **Meditation with The Strength and The Sun:** After the bath, meditate with the Tarot cards The Strength (arcanum 8) and The Sun (arcanum 19). The Strength represents inner strength, determination, and the ability to overcome obstacles. The Sun symbolizes success, abundance, vitality, and recognition. Visualize how these energies intensify within you, guiding you towards the fulfillment of your goals.

5. **Gratitude and action:** Give thanks for the opportunities that already exist in your life and for those that are to come. Visualize your goals of success, fame, and leadership with clarity and determination. Take action to turn your desires into reality.

Additional tips:

- You can add inspiring music or nature sounds during the bath to create an atmosphere conducive to meditation and energetic connection.

- If you don't have fresh rose petals, you can use dried petals or rose essence.

- You can repeat this ritual every month to keep the energy of success, fame, and leadership flowing in your life.

- May this ritual help you shine with your own light, attract the success, fame, and leadership you desire, and conquer the love of others!

Autumn Equinox Ritual for Harmony, Reconciliation, and Love

Objective: To harness the energy of the autumn equinox in Libra to perform a ritual that favors harmony, reconciliations, marriage, the resolution of legal matters, and the creation of positive partnerships.

Ideal Moment: Night of September 22nd, when the Sun enters Libra and the energy of balance, justice, and love intensifies.

Materials:

- Pink roses
- Rose quartz
- Water with honey (a small amount)
- Pink candle
- Tarot cards Justice (arcanum 11) and The Empress (arcanum 3)
- Small bag

Preparation:

Creating a harmonious space: On a table, place a circle of pink roses, symbolizing love, harmony, and union. In the center of the circle, place the rose quartz previously washed with water and honey, to purify it and enhance its energy. On top of the quartz, place a pink candle.

Lighting the flame of harmony: Light the pink candle and let its light illuminate the space, creating an atmosphere of peace and tranquility. Allow the candle to burn completely overnight, symbolizing transformation and the release of negative energies.

Meditation with Justice and The Empress: The next day, meditate with the Tarot cards Justice (arcanum 11) and The Empress (arcanum 3). Justice represents balance, fairness, and conflict resolution. The Empress symbolizes love, creativity, and abundance. Visualize how these energies guide you towards harmony, reconciliation, and the fulfillment of your desires in both personal and professional spheres.

Activating the rose quartz: With your left hand, take the rose quartz and make a wish with clarity and conviction. Pass the quartz to your right hand and say your name once, connecting the energy of the quartz with your being. Store the quartz in a small bag and carry it with you as an amulet that reminds you of the harmonious energy you have activated.

Meaning and benefits:

This ritual helps you attract harmony to your relationships, both personal and professional.

It favors reconciliation with people with whom you have had differences.

It increases the chances of finding love and getting married.

It gives you the necessary energy to resolve legal matters in a fair and favorable way.

It drives you to create positive and prosperous partnerships in your life.

Additional tips:

- You can add relaxing music or nature sounds during meditation to deepen the energy connection.
- If you don't have fresh pink roses, you can use dried petals or rose essence.
- You can repeat this ritual whenever you need to attract harmony, reconciliation, or love into your life.
- Remember that this ritual is a tool complementary to your own personal effort to achieve happiness and well-being.
- May this ritual help you cultivate harmony within yourself and attract love, justice, and prosperity into your life!

Autumn Equinox Ritual for Harmony, Reconciliation, and Love: Closing Cycles and Embracing Transformation: Farewelling the Old and Embracing the New

Objective: To harness the transformative energy of the Sun in Scorpio to perform a ritual that allows you to close cycles, leave behind what no longer serves you, and open yourself to new opportunities in your life.

Ideal Moment: Night of October 22nd, when the Sun is in Scorpio, intensifying the energy of transformation, death, and rebirth.

Materials:

- Large bag or sack
- Items that no longer serve you (clothes, objects, etc.)
- Tarot card The Death (arcanum 13)

Preparation:

Letting go of the past: On the night of October 22nd, take some time to select all those items that no longer serve you, that have fulfilled their cycle in your life and that only occupy physical and mental space. Clothes that you no longer wear, objects that no longer bring you joy, memories that tie you to the past... everything that no longer vibrates with you must be released.

Meditation with The Death: Before bed, meditate with the Tarot card The Death (arcanum 13). This card does not represent physical death, but transformation, the end of one stage and the beginning of another. Visualize how you let go of what no longer serves you, opening space for the new, fresh, and positive that is about to come.

Saying goodbye to the old: On the morning of October 23rd, take the sack or bag you have prepared and fill it with all the items you have selected to leave behind. Leave your house with determination and find a quiet place in nature, away from noise and distractions.

Releasing the burden: In that quiet place, say goodbye to each of the objects you are going to release. Thank them for what they brought you at the time and recognize that they have already fulfilled their function. Visualize how their energy is released and transformed into something new and positive for you.

A new beginning: Leave the sack in the chosen place and walk away without looking back. Trust that what no longer serves you is gone forever, freeing up space for the new and wonderful to come into your life.

Meaning and benefits:

This ritual helps you close emotional, sentimental, and material cycles that prevent you from moving forward in your life.

It allows you to get rid of the burden of the past, freeing up space for personal renewal and growth.

It opens the doors to new opportunities, positive relationships, and experiences.

It connects you with the transformative energy of Scorpio, urging you to be reborn and reinvent yourself.

Additional tips:

- You can add relaxing music or nature sounds during meditation to deepen the energy connection.
- If you wish, you can write a farewell letter to the objects you are going to leave behind, expressing your emotions and thanking them for what they have brought you.
- You can perform this ritual every time you feel the need to close a cycle and open yourself to new possibilities.
- Remember that this ritual is a tool complementary to your own personal effort to achieve well-being and fulfillment.

- May this ritual help you close cycles with peace and determination, to free yourself from the past and open yourself to transformation and rebirth in your life!